T0328585

Cambridge Elements ☰

Elements in the Philosophy of Mathematics
edited by
Penelope Rush
University of Tasmania
Stewart Shapiro
The Ohio State University

THE MEREOLOGY OF CLASSES

Gabriel Uzquiano
University of Southern California

CAMBRIDGE
UNIVERSITY PRESS

Shaftesbury Road, Cambridge CB2 8EA, United Kingdom

One Liberty Plaza, 20th Floor, New York, NY 10006, USA

477 Williamstown Road, Port Melbourne, VIC 3207, Australia

314–321, 3rd Floor, Plot 3, Splendor Forum, Jasola District Centre,
New Delhi – 110025, India

103 Penang Road, #05–06/07, Visioncrest Commercial, Singapore 238467

Cambridge University Press is part of Cambridge University Press & Assessment,
a department of the University of Cambridge.

We share the University's mission to contribute to society through the pursuit of
education, learning and research at the highest international levels of excellence.

www.cambridge.org
Information on this title: www.cambridge.org/9781009500975

DOI: 10.1017/9781009092241

When citing this work, please include a reference to the DOI 10.1017/9781009092241

First published 2024

A catalogue record for this publication is available from the British Library.

ISBN 978-1-009-50097-5 Hardback
ISBN 978-1-009-09641-6 Paperback
ISSN 2399-2883 (online)
ISSN 2514-3808 (print)

The Mereology of Classes

Elements in the Philosophy of Mathematics

DOI: 10.1017/9781009092241
First published online: May 2024

Gabriel Uzquiano
University of Southern California

Author for correspondence: Gabriel Uzquiano, uzquiano@usc.edu

Abstract: This Element is a systematic study of the question of whether classes are composed of further parts. Mereology is the theory of the relation of part to whole, and the Element will ask how that relation applies to classes. One reason the issue has received attention in the literature is the hope that a clear picture of the mereology of classes may provide further insights into the foundations of set theory. The Element will consider two main perspectives on the mereology of classes on which classes are indeed composed of further parts. They, however, disagree as to the identity of those parts. Each perspective admits more than one implementation, and one of the purposes of this Element is to explain what is at stake with each choice.

Keywords: mereology, classes, plural quantification, set theory, part–whole

ISBNs: 9781009500975 (HB), 9781009096416 (PB), 9781009092241 (OC)
ISSNs: 2399-2883 (online), 2514-3808 (print)

Contents

1 Introduction

One object may be composed of parts – a computer is composed of a motherboard, a central processing unit, and a hard drive. These material objects are parts of the computer, and the computer is a sum of these parts. Computers are material artifacts, but the question of whether an object is composed of parts seems to make sense across ontological categories. The performance of a play is an event composed of acts, which are, in turn, composed of scenes. Organisms are composed of parts, some of which perform specific biological functions: a heart is part of the circulatory system, which is itself part of some organisms. Perhaps more controversial is the question of whether abstract objects such as sentences – and the propositions they express – are composed of parts. We speak of sentences as composed of words, whose written articulations are, in turn, composed of letters. And, similarly, when a sentence expresses a proposition, we may be tempted to speak of the proposition as composed of parts that correspond to parts of the sentence. On this view, propositions themselves are complex, and their mereological structure mirrors that of the sentences that express them. Others take propositions to be truth conditions, which they identify with sets of possible worlds. The proposition that Socrates is a philosopher is, on this view, the set of possible worlds at which Socrates is a philosopher. But even then, if the set of possible worlds at which Socrates is a philosopher is part of the set of worlds at which he is human, then the proposition that Socrates is human should be part of the proposition that Socrates is a philosopher.

One common reaction to these questions is to dismiss them on the grounds that the relation of part to whole doesn't properly apply to abstract objects such as sentences or propositions. Instead, the relation of part should be restricted to the domain of material objects, spatiotemporal regions, events, and the like. On this view, we should construe talk of parts of sentences or propositions as nonliteral or as a figure of speech. More generally, there is no genuine question as to whether a given object is composed when the object in question lies outside the sphere of material objects, spatiotemporal regions, events, and the like.

That is not the stance we take in this Element. Instead, we assume that the relation of part to whole may be properly applied across ontological categories. In that respect, parthood is not unlike identity: much like each and every object is self-identical, each and every object is at the very least part of itself. It is, of course, a further question whether they are invariably composed of further parts. Even if we grant that propositions are parts of themselves, the question arises of whether we should conceive of them as composed of further parts.

We may consider ordinary judgments as evidence for the claim that sentences – or propositions – are composed of further parts, but it is a substantive question whether ordinary uses of the word 'part' should be taken at face value or whether at least some of them should instead be construed as nonliteral or as a figure of speech. We speak of a complex number as composed of a real part and an imaginary part, but it is not at all obvious that we should take all such talk at face value. We similarly describe a proof as composed of steps, a sphere as composed of two hemispheres, and a book as composed of chapters. That we do this is uncontroversial, and the question now is whether we should take all these judgments at face value. But whatever we do, we have taken the view that we should not discard the literal interpretation just because the objects in question are not material or they lack spatiotemporal location.

Let us now distinguish the question of whether the relation of part to whole applies across ontological categories from the further question of whether there is more than one way in which an object may be part of another. One may be tempted to distinguish the way in which a heart is part of a body from the way in which the letter 'a' is part of the written word 'part'. And if one does this, it is presumably an open question whether the relation of part to whole is subject to different constraints relative to different domains of application. That is, one should not take for granted that the part-to-whole relation on the domain of set theory is subject to the same principles as the relation is on the domain of material objects.

We will use the label *compositional pluralism* for the general hypothesis that a variety of different relations may constitute the relation of part to whole across domains of application. A compositional pluralist may want to distinguish the way in which an arm is part of a body from the way in which a word is part of a sentence; the way in which a propositional constituent may be part of a proposition; and the way in which a member may be part of a set. These relations are all ways in which an object may be part of another, but they may be subject to different constraints and there is no reason to expect all of them to abide by the axioms of classical mereology. Kit Fine provides a sustained defense of the outlook in Fine (2010) but Armstrong (1991) and Johnston (2006) are further examples.

We contrast this view with *compositional monism* according to which there is a uniform sense in which an object is part of another across ontological categories. There is just one basic relation of part to whole across domains, which is often construed as the subject matter of classical mereology. This is, for example, the perspective David Lewis adopts in Lewis (1991).[1] One may

---

[1] See Cotnoir and Varzi (2021) for discussion.

advance the axioms of classical mereology as perfectly general hypotheses governing the part-to-whole relation across different domains of application.

We now turn to the question of whether mathematical objects, be they numbers, sets, functions, algebras, graphs, geometric figures, or spaces, are composed of parts. We speak of a complex number as composed of a real part and an imaginary part; we describe the additive group of integers as part of the ring of integers; we speak of a first-order subtheory, for example, Robinson's arithmetic, as a part of another theory, for example, Peano arithmetic; we refer to the vertices of a triangle as parts of its boundary; and we speak of the two separate parts of a hyperbola. Indeed, the part-to-whole relation makes an explicit appearance in the subject in Euclid's axioms, the fifth of which reads that the whole is greater than the part.[2] More generally, Bell (2004) makes clear how talk of part is central to mathematical practice in a wide array of areas from algebra and geometry to functional analysis, topology, and category theory.

Given the stance we have just taken, the question of whether mathematical objects are composed of parts may be thought to be trivial. Mathematical objects are no exception to the hypothesis that the relation of part to whole applies unrestrictedly across ontological categories: mathematical objects are, at a minimum, part of themselves. The more substantive question is whether they may be composed of *proper* parts, where by a *proper part* of an object, we mean a part other than the object itself. And if they are, then what exactly are their proper parts?

We speak of mathematical objects as composed of proper parts, but as we mentioned earlier, the crucial question is whether such talk should be taken at face value in mathematics or whether it should instead be construed as non-literal, as a figure of speech, or even as a powerful heuristic.[3] Maybe there is no blanket answer to this question, especially given the great variety and diversity of uses of 'part' and 'whole' in mathematics. Maybe some of them are nothing but a powerful heuristic, and maybe others should be taken literally as instances of the part-to-whole relation in certain mathematical domains.

This work focuses on the case of classes, and the question of whether to allow for them to be composed of proper parts. After we explain the reasons for the focus on classes, two broad perspectives will emerge as candidate answers to the question of what exactly are the parts of a class. While the two perspectives are, strictly speaking, orthogonal to the question of compositional monism, one of them will align with compositional monism and take the answer to that question to be constrained by the hypothesis that the relation of part to whole

---

[2] The fifth axiom as opposed to the fifth postulate better known as the parallel postulate.

[3] That is how we read Bell (2004).

abides by the axioms of classical mereology. The other perspective is compatible with either view, but it will require a weaker mereological framework.

2 The Mereology of Classes

We have raised the question of whether mathematical objects are ever literally composed of proper parts, but we now confine our discussion to the case of classes. The reason we speak of classes rather than sets is not because we envisage some fundamental ontological distinction between them. We remain neutral on the question of whether *nonempty* sets should be considered as special cases of classes. That is, for all we write, there are, in addition to sets, classes that are not sets. Some theories of classes such as von Neumann–Bernays–Gödel (NBG) class theory or Morse–Kelley (MK) class theory posit *proper* classes, which are not coextensive with a set, whereas standard set theory, by which we mean Zermelo–Fraenkel set theory with the axiom of choice (ZFC), does not. We will similarly speak of *individuals* to refer to objects without members. We adopt the stipulation laid down in Lewis (1991) according to which classes have members. That means that the empty set is not a class and requires special treatment. No matter; for present purposes, we may identify it with a chosen individual that is not a class.

There are many reasons for the focus on the question of whether classes are composed of proper parts. One reason is related to the broader question of whether mathematical objects are ever composed of proper parts. To the extent to which vast areas of mathematics reduce to the theory of classes – or set theory in the absence of proper classes – the relevant mathematical objects are identified with classes, and the question of whether they are composed of proper parts reduces to the question of whether certain classes are, in turn, composed of further parts. We may vindicate the claim that Robinson's arithmetic is part of Peano arithmetic when we identify each with a suitable set of formulas. And we may similarly take at face value the assertion that a hyperbola has two separate parts when we identify it with an appropriate set of Cartesian coordinates. So, the question of whether classes are composed of proper parts may play a central role in the discussion of the broader question of whether mathematical objects more generally are composed of proper parts.

The next reason is related to the first. Once we take classes to be composed of proper parts, the question arises whether distinctive class-theoretic relations such as membership or the subclass relation submit to a mereological analysis. That is, the question is whether we should expect class-theoretic relations to be definable in terms of the relation of part to whole. This question is paramount for those who harbor foundational hopes for mereology. Indeed, Leśniewski (1999) and Leśniewski (1927) originally billed mereology as a nominalistically accept-able replacement for set theory, one whose success depends on its ability to replicate a rich variety of class-theoretic facts within the framework. The prospects for such a project are not too bright: Urbaniak (2014) and Simons (1987) offer an assessment of some of its limitations.

But even if we set aside those nominalistic scruples, the question remains whether we may eventually be in a position to reduce the theory of classes to mereology if we side with one or another specification of the parts of a class. One may, in other words, hope to be able to provide a mereological character-ization of the class-theoretic universe and the relation of member to class. That would in turn allow one to faithfully interpret a variety of mathematical structures in mereology, which would, in turn, raise the prospects of a mereo-logical foundation for vast areas of mathematics. That expectation, however, will turn out to be unreasonable no matter how one specifies the parts of a class on the main perspectives under consideration in this Element.[4]

The next motivation for the focus on the question of how the part-to-whole relation is supposed to apply to classes is that the answer may help us confront a difficult problem in the foundations of set theory. That is the problem of *proper classes*, which are often described as setlike objects that are too large to form a set. Proper classes appear to play an important role in set theory. They enable us to provide finite axiomatizations of set theory, and they seem to be a crucial ingredient for the formulation of certain large cardinal hypotheses.[5] The problem of proper classes is the challenge to provide an account of the distinction between sets and proper classes, which, on the one hand, makes classes sufficiently different from sets, and, on the other, provides some assur-ance that classes are as real and well-defined as sets are. Horsten (2016) and Horsten and Welch (2016) have recently proposed conceiving of proper classes as *parts* of the set-theoretic universe, which is, in turn, conceived as a sum of all sets. On their view, the mereology of classes provides a solution to a persistent problem in the foundations of set theory.

One more reason for the focus on classes is that there appears to be abundant linguistic evidence for the thesis that classes may be composed of further parts even if that evidence appears to pull us in different directions. On the one hand, Kit Fine and Mark Johnston, for example, Fine (2010) and Johnston (2006), remind us that we generally describe a set – and a class – as composed of its members, which are *contained in* it. That would seem to suggest sets – and

---

[4] The problem is compounded by the observation that classical mereology, for example, is decid-able since Hamkins and Kikuchi (2016) argue that no decidable theory is able to formalize arithmetic and be Δ_0-sound.

[5] See Uzquiano (2003) and Horsten and Welch (2016) for discussion.

classes more generally – have their members as parts. On the other hand, we seem to speak of the subclasses of a class as parts of it; indeed, as David Lewis reminds us in Lewis (1991), the German word for subset, 'Teilmenge' is literally 'set-part' and that pioneers like Cantor and Zermelo often employed 'Teil' which is literally 'part' for the subset relation, sometimes with the implication that the subset has members. None of this is conclusive; none of the theorists we mentioned take all such uses at face value. Instead, they each dismiss *some* of these uses of 'part' as metaphorical or nonliteral or as a mere reflection of the analogy between part and a nonmereological relation.

One last reason for the focus on classes is more pragmatic in character: unlike the broader question of whether mathematical objects ever submit to a decomposition into proper parts, the question of classes has received a great deal of attention in recent literature, and more progress is to be expected with respect to that question than with respect to the broader, less manageable question of whether mathematical objects in general may be composed of proper parts.[6]

Simple Classes

We have taken for granted that classes are parts of themselves, but it is a further question whether they may, in fact, have parts other than themselves. The question may seem ill-posed. Some classes seem rather complex and you may expect them to come with an abundance of proper parts. While the two main perspectives we discuss in this Element make allowance for classes to be composed of proper parts, we will use this section to outline a perspective on which we should remain agnostic on this question. Nothing in the mathematics of classes requires them to have parts other than themselves.

One option is to decline to construe the complexity of classes as a species of mereological complexity. Instead, one may deny that class-theoretic relations such as that of subclass or member are in fact to be analyzed in terms of the relation of part to whole. This notwithstanding the existence of formal parallels between some of these relations and that of part. The subclass relation, for example, is reflexive, antisymmetric, and transitive, which means that it forms a partial order much like the relation of part is often supposed to do. But of course, not all partial orders are mereological relations, and the view under consideration is one on which the subclass relation is *not* a special case of the relation of part to whole.

---

[6] Explicit discussion of the case of classes may be found in Armstrong (1991), Lewis (1991), Lewis (1993), Bigelow (1993), Forrest (2002a), Forrest (2002b), Johnston (2006), Caplan, Tillman, and Reeder (2010), and Hamkins and Kikuchi (2016).

Or one could conceive of classes as *proxies* for their members – much like a Fregean extension, for example, is an object conceived as a stand-in for a Fregean concept. We needn't regard the relation between the extension of the concept and its instances as a mereological relation; there is no sense in which horses are parts of the extension of the Fregean concept *horse*. One may still ask whether the proxies in question, much like the extension of the concept *horse*, may come with proper parts of their own, but the important point is that nothing in their role as proxies for their members requires them to have proper parts. So, there is no reason to expect substantive generalizations to underwrite a systematic mereology of classes.

The outlook is not unprecedented, but rather a view Cartwright (2001) intimate when they suggest that the subject matter of set theory is the relation of *representation* a set bears to several objects. While Cartwright (2001) are not directly concerned with the question of whether sets themselves are composed of parts, it seems clear that nothing in the role they play requires the relevant relation of representation to submit to a mereological characterization. To claim that a class $\{a, b\}$ *represents* the objects a and b is perfectly consistent with the mereological simplicity of the class: there is no reason to expect a mereological analysis of the relation of representation. The outlook is similarly explored in Uzquiano (2015a) as an alternative to more traditional conceptions of sets as ontologically dependent on their members. The crucial thought is that nothing in the mathematical role classes are designed to play requires them to have parts other than themselves.

That general stance would align well with the eliminativist form of structuralism McGee (1997) advances. One assumes the existence of a binary relation that satisfies the axioms of ZFC and construes set-theoretic claims as generalizations over such binary relations. Each such binary relation allows us to conceive of a class as a proxy for its members, but the identity or mereological composition of the proxy is, in fact, irrelevant for mathematical purposes. That means, in particular, that it is unimportant whether we take classes to include other classes as parts. What matters is that a system of classes satisfies the axioms of set theory, and so whether mereological atoms or complex sums play the role of classes is completely immaterial. Similar remarks apply to modal formulations of eliminative structuralism such as Hellman (1989) and Hellman (1996).

Nor is the hypothesis that classes are composed of further parts required to make sense of the iterative conception of set in line with the minimalist approach Incurvati (2020) outlines. The minimalist program takes the iterative conception of set as boiling down to the thought that sets are objects that collectively exemplify the structure of the cumulative hierarchy, whether they are mereologically simple or complex. Matters would be different, of course, if we found the hypothesis that classes have proper parts to be fruitful in other respects, and this is one dimension of comparison we will consider when we introduce the two perspectives under discussion in this Element.

Parts of Classes

Let us set aside the hypothesis that classes are simple proxies for their members. If a class is composed of *proper parts*, then it is a *sum* of proper parts, that is, parts that are different from the sum.[7] Talk of 'sum' is highly suggestive, but following Forrest (2002b), there is more than one formal explication of *sum* in terms of part. Consider, for example, the contrast between *fusion* and *join*. To say that an object is a *fusion* of some parts is to say that it has each of them as parts, and anything that overlaps the object overlaps at least one of the parts.[8] Nothing else is built on this characterization of fusion. To say that an object is a *join* of some parts is to say that it has them as parts and that it is itself part of anything that has them as parts, or, in other words, it is a minimal upper bound under the part-to-whole relation. This contrast will eventually become important, but notice that there are other characterizations of sum in the offing. For example, yet another way to conceive of the sum of some parts is as whatever object overlaps exactly those parts, which is what Cotnoir and Varzi (2021) call a *Goodman fusion*.

Whatever explication we choose, the thesis that classes are sums is not very informative unless we are in a position to specify their parts. We will discuss two rival approaches to the question of what exactly are the parts of a class. One option is to identify the parts of a class with its subclasses in line with the linguistic evidence David Lewis mentions in Lewis (1991). One consequence of this approach is that classes are, in fact, *not* composed of their members; they do not often include their members as parts. The alternative approach is to construe classes as composed of their members, but since the relation of part to whole is presumably transitive, the parts of these members are themselves parts of the class. The parts of a class thus include its members, the members of its members, the members of the members of its members, and so on.

We will devote later sections to explore each approach in more detail. For now, we will content ourselves with an outline of their broad contours.

The Main Thesis

Both Lewis (1991) and Lewis (1993) target a theory of sets and classes that is generally known as Morse–Kelley set theory (MK), one whose variables range over individuals and classes. Lewis uses the term 'class' to apply to classes *with*

---

[7] Some conceive of singleton classes as simple classes without further parts.

[8] To say that two objects overlap is, as usual, to say that they have at least one part in common.

members and construes the *empty set* as a chosen individual. Sets with members are special cases of classes, which are contrasted with *proper* classes. In addition to this, he is a compositional monist for whom there is no significant difference between the way in which a subclass is part of a class and the way in which a motherboard, say, is part of a computer. There is just one basic relation of part to whole, which applies across ontological categories in accordance with the axioms of classical mereology.

Lewis (1991, 7) defends a succinct answer to the question of what exactly are the parts of a class:

The Main Thesis The parts of a class are all and only its subclasses.

That is, for something to be a part of a class is for it to be a subclass of it. David Lewis arrives at the thesis that the parts of a class are exactly its subclasses in two steps.

There is, first, the First Thesis:

The First Thesis One class is part of another if, and only if, the first is a subclass of the second.[9]

Even if classes are members of other classes, they will not constitute a part of another class unless they are a subclass of it. That is, while the class $\{a\}$ is a member of the class $\{\{a\}, b\}$, the former is *not* a part of the latter because it is not one of its subclasses. Given the stipulation that classes have members, and the subsequent decision to classify the empty set as an individual rather than a class, notice that nothing in the letter of the thesis requires the empty set to be itself part of a class.

The First Thesis leaves open whether a class may include further parts as well. Lewis' Second Thesis settles that question:

The Second Thesis No class has any part that is not a class.[10]

We list all the parts of a given class once we list all of its subclasses: $\{\{a\}\}$, $\{\{b\}\}$, and $\{\{a\}, \{b\}\}$ exhaust the parts of $\{\{a\}, \{b\}\}$. Notice that neither $\{a\}$ nor the empty set are parts of that class: $\{a\}$ is not part of it because it is not a subclass but rather a member of $\{\{a\}, \{b\}\}$. The empty set, on the other hand, is not a part of that class because it is not, in fact, a class, given our stipulation that all classes have members.

Lewis derives the Main Thesis from the two theses, but he is careful to mount an argument for the Second Thesis on the basis of more basic mereological hypotheses (on which more later).

---

[9] See Lewis (1991, 4).   [10] See Lewis (1991, 6).

Whatever we think of Lewis' arguments for the Main Thesis, we should acknowledge one important limitation. For given the Main Thesis, we are not in a position to characterize membership in terms of part. The Main Thesis tells us that a class has a decomposition into singletons, which are mereologically simple. To the extent to which they lack further mereological structure, they remain a black box from a strictly mereological standpoint: they are mereologically indiscernible, which means that mereological structure alone will not help us uncover which objects are members of which singletons. One could in principle exchange the contents of these singletons conceived as black boxes from a mereological perspective without making a difference with respect to the relation of part to whole. The exchange would, however, interfere with the relation a member bears to a class.

These informal considerations translate into a more precise observation Joel Hamkins and Makoto Kikuchi record in Hamkins and Kikuchi (2016, theorem 2). It is clear that $\subseteq$ is definable in terms of $\in$. If $\langle V, \in \rangle$ is a model of ZFC, we define the relation $\subseteq$ on V as usual: $x \subseteq y := \forall z (z \in x \rightarrow z \in y)$. But the question now is whether we may conversely define $\in$ in terms of $\subseteq$. To refute this claim, we may rely on the general observation that an automorphism on a structure $\langle V, \subseteq \rangle$ will preserve relations that are definable in $\langle V, \subseteq \rangle$. By an *automorphism* τ of $\langle V, \subseteq \rangle$, we mean, as usual, an isomorphism of the structure onto itself. That is, τ is a one-to-one map from V to V that *preserves* $\subseteq$, that is, $\tau(x) \subseteq \tau(y)$ whenever $x \subseteq y$. It is routine to check that given such an automorphism τ of $\langle V, \subseteq \rangle$, if a binary relation R is definable in $\langle V, \subseteq \rangle$, then we have that for all $x, y \in V$, xRy if, and only if, $\tau(x)R\tau(y)$.[11] But given a model of ZFC $\langle V, \in \rangle$, we may produce an automorphism τ of $\langle V, \subseteq \rangle$ which does *not* preserve $\in$. That is, there are $x, y \in V$ such that $x \in y$ even though $\tau(x) \notin \tau(y)$. Unfortunately, given a model of ZFC $\langle V, \in \rangle$, we may produce an automorphism τ of $\langle V, \subseteq \rangle$ which does *not* preserve $\in$. That is, there are $x, y \in V$ such that $x \in y$ even though $\tau(x) \notin \tau(y)$.

Proposition 1.1 (Hamkins and Kikuchi) There is no definition of $\in$ in terms of $\subseteq$.

Proof Outline Given a model of ZFC of the form $\langle V, \in \rangle$, we produce an automorphism τ of $\langle V, \subseteq \rangle$, which is *not* an automorphism of $\langle V, \in \rangle$. Let θ be a permutation of V that exchanges $\emptyset$ with $\{\emptyset\}$ but leaves every other set unchanged. Define $\tau : V \rightarrow V$ such that $\tau(x) = \{\theta(y) : y \in x\}$. Since θ is a

---

[11] If $\varphi(x,y)$ defines R in $\langle V, \subseteq \rangle$, then it suffices to note that $\langle V, \subseteq \rangle \vDash \varphi(x,y)$ if and only if $\langle V, \subseteq \rangle \vDash \varphi(\tau(x), \tau(y))$.

permutation of V, τ is an automorphism on $\langle V, \subseteq \rangle$: $x \subseteq y$ if and only if $\{\theta(z) : z \in x\} \subseteq \{\theta(z) : z \in y\}$ if and only if $\tau(x) \subseteq \tau(y)$. But τ does *not* preserve $\in$. For notice that although $\varnothing \in \{\varnothing\}$, $\tau(\varnothing) \notin \tau(\{\varnothing\})$. On the one hand, $\tau(\varnothing) = \varnothing$, which is the set of θ-images of members of $\varnothing$. But on the other hand, $\tau(\{\varnothing\}) = \{\theta(\varnothing)\}$, which is none other than $\{\{\varnothing\}\}$. Since $\varnothing \notin \{\{\varnothing\}\}$, we conclude that $\tau(\varnothing) \notin \tau(\{\varnothing\})$. It follows that τ is an automorphism of $\langle V, \subseteq \rangle$ that does *not* preserve membership.

More generally, Hamkins and Kikuchi explain how to make changes in the relation $\in$ of a model of ZFC $\langle V, \in \rangle$ while preserving the same subclass relation. Given a definable nontrivial permutation θ of V, one may define $x \in^\theta y$ as $\theta(x) \in y$ and note that $x \subseteq^\theta y$ if, and only if, $x \subseteq y$ —even though it is *not* the case that $x \in^\theta y$ if, and only if, $x \in y$. There is nothing special about ZFC, and it is not difficult to verify that the observation generalizes to cover models of theories of classes such as NBG and MK.

The moral seems inescapable: if the Main Thesis is true, then *neither* set theory *nor* the theory of classes reduces to mereology alone. We do better to supplement the language of mereology with a primitive singleton operation governed by its own distinctive axioms. Hamkins and Kikuchi acknowledge, for example, that the member relation remains definable in terms of subclass and singleton. They prove, in particular, that a model of set theory $\langle V, \in \rangle$ is interdefinable with the model $\langle V, \subseteq, \sigma \rangle$, where σ is the singleton operator $\sigma : a \mapsto \{a\}$, which maps an object to its singleton.[12] This observation opens the door to a broad research program, whose goal is to reduce class theory to the combination of mereology and a theory of singletons.

David Lewis had implemented the program in Lewis (1991), but the extent to which the framework provides a foundation for class theory is sensitive to one's attitude toward the singleton operation. One option is to attempt to identify singletons with more familiar objects to which we may have independent epistemic access. David Armstrong, for example, identifies singletons with certain states of affairs in Armstrong (1991), and John Bigelow similarly identifies them with haecceities in Bigelow (1993).[13] Other candidates are not difficult to isolate: self-identity tropes in the manner of D. C. Williams, tropes (Forrest 2002a), and rigid embodiments (Caplan, Tillman, and Reeder 2010).[14] In contrast to this, David Lewis dismisses the prospects of a reduction of

---

[12] This is theorem 13 of Hamkins and Kikuchi (2016).

[13] However, Bigelow departs from the Main Thesis to the extent to which he proceeds to identify sets with plural haecceities as opposed to sums of singular haecceities. The point remains that a proponent of the Main Thesis could still make use of the identification of singletons with singular haecceities.

[14] The identification of singletons with rigid embodiments fits better with an alternative conception of how classes enter into the part–whole relation.

singletons to more familiar objects on the grounds that they either involve what he regards as unmereological modes of composition or remain profoundly mysterious. Instead, he posits the existence of an operation, which satisfies certain structural axioms from which we can deduce the basic principles of Morse–Kelley class theory.

Hierarchical Composition

One apparently untoward consequence of the Main Thesis is that classes are not composed of their members, which is how we often describe them. We often talk of the members as contained in the class to which they belong, which again suggests that they are regarded as parts. Subscribers to the Main Thesis will presumably construe such talk as nonliteral or as a figure of speech, one that is perhaps grounded in an analogy between member and the relation some *atoms* bear to the sum they compose. Suggestive as the analogy may be, they may continue, we shouldn't read too much into it.

One more argument against the hypothesis that classes are composed of members is that unlike part, the member relation is neither reflexive nor transitive: a is a member of $\{a\}$, which is a member of $\{\{a\}\}$, but a is not a member of $\{\{a\}\}$. To the extent to which the part-to-whole relation should form a partial order, that is, be reflexive, antisymmetric, and transitive, we have reason to reject the identification of part and member. That isn't, however, a decisive consideration against the hypothesis that classes have their members as parts. For the suggestion is not that we identify part and member, but rather that we regard cases of membership as special cases of part. Classes exhibit, in fact, a hierarchical mereological structure: they include its members as *immediate parts*, but they may include other parts as well, for example, members of their members, members of the members of their members, and so on. In other words, the proper parts of a class would include whatever stands in the ancestral of the relation of immediate part to it. These may include classes and *individuals*, which are objects without members, and while the immediate parts of classes are members, the immediate parts of individuals are not.[15]

Classes are not the exception but rather the rule. Our body is a complex material object composed of limbs and organs, but these are complex material objects themselves composed of bones and tissue. Even if we count limbs and organs as immediate parts of the body, the bones and tissues that compose these are not immediate parts of the body but rather are mere parts of it. The parts of

---

[15] One object, as usual, x stands in the *ancestral* of a binary relation R to another object y if, and only if, there is a *finite* sequence $x_1, \ldots, x_n$ such that xRx_1, for each $i < n$, x_iRx_{i+1}, and x_nRy.

a body would include not only its immediate parts, but the immediate parts of those, the immediate parts of the immediate parts of those, and so on. While the relation of *immediate part* is not reflexive or transitive, the reflexive closure of the ancestral of that relation is in fact a partial order, for example, reflexive, antisymmetric, and transitive. So, the reflexive closure of the ancestral of immediate part is a candidate relation of part, for example, Fine (1999, p. 563).[16] This is not to say we should expect this relation to abide by the axioms of classical mereology. Proponents of the hierarchical perspective will depart from classical mereology at crucial junctures, which result in a rather different account of the relation of part to whole. Different variations on the hierarchical outlook are outlined in Fine (1999), Johnston (2006), and Koslicki (2008).[17]

Classes are particularly amenable to the hierarchical perspective. To be sure, each class is part of itself, but in addition to this, each class contains each of its members as an immediate part. Since immediate parts are parts, and the part–whole relation is transitive, each class contains the members of its members as further parts. In other words, the parts of a class include that very class, its members, the members of its members, the members of the members of its members, and so on. Furthermore, if some of these parts are individuals, then the class includes the parts of these individuals as well.

We have implicitly restricted attention to the hierarchical mereological structure of *impure* classes generated from a given domain of individuals, but it is not obvious how to model *pure* classes on this approach. For whatever we make of the empty set, it should *not* have members as immediate parts. One option at this point is to follow Lewis (1991) and conceive of the empty set as a chosen individual without immediate parts. The choice would be arbitrary: there is no reason to prefer one individual to another to encode the existence of a set without members. While that is our preference in this Element, there are other alternatives in the market: Johnston (2006) suggests the identification of the empty set with the singleton of an *arbitrary* item, one that is no object in particular. The thought is that there would be no item in particular that would be a member of the empty set as desired. On the other hand, Caplan, Tillman, and Reeder (2010) propose to identify the empty set with a certain attribute, one they take to unify the immediate parts of a class. So, the empty set is not a class but rather an attribute, which, for them, is part of each and every class.

---

[16] The *reflexive closure* of a relation on a set is the $\subseteq$-least relation that includes R and is reflexive on that set. Antisymmetry requires a separate argument.

[17] More recently, Goodman (2022) explicitly combines the vision with a plenitudinous ontology.

Before we continue the discussion of the hierarchical approach, let us codify the first pass at the hierarchical perspective on classes:

Hierarchical Composition The immediate parts of a class are all and only its members. The parts of a class are the class itself and all and only its ancestral immediate parts.

The parts of a class include the class itself, its members, the members of its members, the members of the members of its members, and so on. If some of those members are nonclasses, their immediate parts will be parts of the class as well.

The letter of Hierarchical Composition is neutral with respect to whether immediate part should be taken as basic or whether it should be explained in terms of a more basic relation of part. We have already intimated one reason to prefer the latter option: to the extent to which one may expect the most basic relation of part to form a partial order, one has reason to rule immediate part as the more basic relation of part. While members are parts of classes, being a member is not a basic way of being a part. We will eventually consider an alternative outlook on which we would do better if we adopted immediate part as basic and explained part in terms of it.

One may be tempted to take the further step to regard a class as a sum of its members. It is important to note, however, that the further step is not compulsory: in line with Forrest (2002b), one may subscribe to the letter of Hierarchical Composition and nonetheless deny that a singleton $\{a\}$, for example, is a sum of its sole member on the grounds that a itself – as opposed to the singleton – is the join of the sole proper part of $\{a\}$. They will, in fact, note that a class is *more than the sum of its proper parts*.

Others may operate with a conception of sum on which classes are indeed sums of their members. But notice that it is part of the hierarchical layout that some individuals may in fact compose more than one sum. The molecules that compose a body to the extent to which they exemplify a certain pattern of organization compose a class of molecules, which exists to the extent to which they do and regardless of how they are organized. For a simpler example, three individuals a, b, and c may be the immediate parts of the class $\{a, b, c\}$ as they exist, but they may as well be the immediate parts of a queue as they exemplify a certain spatial arrangement. The difference between the class $\{a, b, c\}$ and the queue a, b and c lies in the fact that the very same three individuals are unified by different *relations* in the words of Fine (1999) or different *principles of unity* in the words of Johnston (2006). One crucial difference between a class of a, b, and c and a queue made out of a, b and c lies in the fact that unlike the latter, the former is guaranteed to exist if the immediate parts exist.

Hierarchical Composition departs from the Main Thesis at least twice over. On the one hand, classes have parts other than its subclasses: in the case of impure classes, they may even include individuals as parts. But on the other hand, and no less importantly, Hierarchical Composition appears to exclude proper subclasses as parts: if a subclass is not an ancestral member of a given class, then it is not part of it, for example, the singleton $\{a\}$ is ruled out as a part of the class $\{a,b\}$. Maybe we should have expected that. Classes are formed out of its members rather than its subclasses, and we should not read too much into the undeniable formal analogy between subclass and part.[18] This is the view Johnston (2006) appears to endorse.

One of the limitations of the Main Thesis, you may recall, is that there is no definition of member exclusively in terms of part. Hierarchical Composition is subject to a similar limitative constraint. To the extent to which one may be inclined to take immediate part as derivative on a more basic relation of part, one may hope to explain membership in terms of that relation of part. Indeed, if we could define *immediate part* in terms of part, we would be able to define membership in terms of part and class; to be a member would just be to be an immediate part of a class.

There is, unfortunately, no optimal characterization of immediate part in terms of part. Simons (1987:108) and Cotnoir and Varzi (2021, sec. 3.3.2) propose to make do with the relation of *maximal proper part*, where one object is a maximal proper part of another if the former is a proper part of the second, and there is no intermediate proper part between them, that is, no object that includes the former as a proper part is a proper part of the latter. For purposes of illustration, on the strict hierarchical view, $\{a\}$, for example, would count as a maximal proper part of $\{\{a\},\{b,c\}\}$, while a would not on the grounds that there is an intermediate proper part between a and $\{\{a\},\{b,c\}\}$, namely, $\{a\}$. So, the tentative definition of immediate part in terms of maximal proper part would allow us to rule out a as an immediate part of $\{\{a\},\{b,c\}\}$. Unfortunately, the characterization of immediate part in terms of maximal proper parts is not without problems. Fine (1992, footnote 16) observes that while a is admittedly an immediate part of $\{a,\{a\}\}$, it is *not* a maximal proper part of $\{a,\{a\}\}$: a is an immediate part of $\{a\}$, which is in turn an immediate part of $\{a,\{a\}\}$.

Kit Fine turned that observation into a formal argument for the thesis that there is no definition of member, $\in$, in terms of its ancestral, which we write $\in^\infty$.[19] It is clear that $\in^\infty$ is definable in terms of $\in$, since to be an ancestral member of a set x is to be a member of its *transitive closure*, which is the $\subseteq$-least set, which

---

[18] Both relations are partial orderings.   [19] For example, $a\in^\infty\{\{a\}\}$, even though $a\notin\{\{a\}\}$.

contains x and contains every member of every member it contains. But since the reflexive closure of $\in^\infty$ corresponds to the more basic relation of part on the view under consideration, we would like to know whether we may conversely define $\in$ in terms of $\in^\infty$. The style of argument we find in Fine (1992, footnote 16) is parallel to the one we used to establish that there is no definition of $\in$ in terms of $\subseteq$. Given a model of ZFC $\langle V, \in \rangle$, we outline an automorphism of $\langle V, \in^\infty \rangle$ that does *not* preserve $\in$. That is, there will be $x, y \in V$ such that $x \in y$ even though $\tau(x) \notin \tau(y)$.

Proposition 1.2 (Fine) There is no definition of $\in$ in terms of its ancestral $\in^\infty$.

Proof Outline Given a model of ZFC of the form $\langle V, \in \rangle$, we seek an automorphism τ of $\langle V, \in^\infty \rangle$ which is not an automorphism on $\langle V, \in \rangle$. Suppose τ is a permutation of V that exchanges $\{ \varnothing, \{ \varnothing \}\}$ with $\{\{ \varnothing \}\}$ in all sets in which they occur.[20] Because τ exchanges each set with another set which has exactly the same ancestral members, the result is, in fact, an automorphism of $\langle V, \in^\infty \rangle$. But τ does *not* preserve $\in$. On the one hand, $\varnothing \in \{ \varnothing, \{ \varnothing \}\}$, but, on the other hand, $\tau(\varnothing) \notin \tau(\{ \varnothing, \{ \varnothing \}\})$, since $\varnothing \notin \{\{ \varnothing \}\}$.

Proponents of Hierarchical Composition face a dilemma. One horn to cope with the indefinability of member in terms of the basic relation of part is to make do with a surrogate for that relation. That would be in line with the direction of travel Forrest (2002b) outlines, even though he hints at a more liberal view of the mereology of classes. The other horn is to invert the order of explanation and to adopt the relation of immediate part as the more basic relation and to explain part in terms of it. Admittedly, immediate part is neither reflexive nor transitive, which many take to disqualify it as a basic way of being a part. But that is no decisive objection for the development of a hierarchical mereology in terms of immediate part within which part is treated as a less basic relation, one which corresponds to the reflexive closure of the ancestral of immediate part. That is at least one interpretation of the project Caplan, Tillman, and Reeder (2010) undertake. They outline a reduction of ZFC against the background of a mereological framework closely related to the theory of embodiments Fine (1999) develops, except that unlike Fine (1999), Caplan, Tillman, and Reeder (2010) explicitly adopt the relation of immediate part as a basic mereological relation.

Hierarchical Composition takes at face value the judgment that classes contain their members as parts, but it ignores the judgment that classes include subclasses as parts. Its proponents are not moved by the structural analogy between the subclass relation and the relation of part to whole, and they

---

[20] For example, $\tau(\{\{ \varnothing \}\}) = \{ \varnothing, \{ \varnothing \}\}$ and $\tau(\{\{\{ \varnothing \}\}\}) = \{\{ \varnothing, \{ \varnothing \}\}\}$.

recommend to construe the latter judgment as nonliteral or as a figure of speech. That is, however, not a compulsory feature of the hierarchical outlook.

One option at this point is to draw a distinction between two different modes of composition in the spirit of compositional pluralism and to suggest that Hierarchical Composition is concerned with just one of them. Once we do this, we have reason to expand the range of parts we ascribe to a class.

Liberal Hierarchical Composition. The immediate parts of a class are the members of the class. The parts of a class are its subclasses and all and only its ancestral immediate parts.

Liberal Hierarchical Composition accommodates the hypothesis that a class may be regarded both as a sum of its members and as a sum of its proper subclasses. Thus $\{\{a\}, b\}$ is, on the one hand, composed of $\{a\}$ and b and, on the other, composed of $\{\{a\}\}$ and $\{b\}$. One difference is that $\{a\}$ and b are immediate parts of the class, whereas $\{\{a\}\}$ and $\{b\}$ are mere parts of it. These modes of composition behave differently: one generates a class as the *union* of its proper subclasses, whereas the other generates it directly from its members. While Fine (2010) takes the first mode of composition as basic and the second as derived, the point remains that there is no unsurmountable obstacle to regarding both the members and the subclasses of a class as parts of that class.

The observation that $\{\{a\}, b\}$ is, on the one hand, composed of $\{a\}$ and b and, on the other, composed of $\{\{a\}\}$ and $\{b\}$ is of a piece with the more general observation that sums are often subject to more than one decomposition into proper parts. Since the relation of proper part is transitive, the picture that emerges is one on which the relation of proper part subsumes chains of member and proper subclass: x would be a proper part of a class y if there is a chain $x_1, \ldots, x_n$, where $x = x_1$, and for each $i < n$, $x_i \in x_{i+1}$ or $x_i \subset x_{i+1}$, and $x_n = y$. The class $\{a\}$, for example, would be a proper part of $\{\{a, b\}, \{c\}\}$, even if the former is itself neither a member nor a subclass of the latter. It is not difficult to verify that the reflexive closure of this relation, which we write $x \preceq y$, is reflexive and transitive.[21] Fine (2010) notes that it takes more work to convince ourselves that the hybrid relation is, in fact, antisymmetric.[22]

---

[21] Reflexivity is trivial. For transitivity, note that if $x \preceq y$ and $y \preceq z$, then, if $x \neq z$, then one chain of member and proper subclass connects x with y or one connects y with z. It is simple to combine these chains into a chain of member and proper subclass that links x with z.

[22] We begin with two preliminary observations. On the one hand, if $x \in y$, then the transitive closure of x is a proper subset of the transitive closure of y. That is, if $x \in y$, then $TC(x) \subset TC(y)$. Furthermore, if $x \subset y$, then $TC(x) \subseteq TC(y)$. It follows that if a suitable chain of member and subset links x and y, $x \preceq y$, then $TC(x) \subseteq TC(y)$. But of course, if $x \neq y$, then $TC(x) \subset TC(y)$, whence $TC(y) \not\subseteq TC(x)$. It follows that $\neg y \preceq x$ as desired.

The prospects of a definition of member in terms of the hybrid of member and proper subclass don't look too bright. For the crucial observation stands that given an individual a, the classes $\{a, \{a\}\}$ and $\{\{a\}\}$ share a and $\{a\}$ as their sole proper parts and, in fact, remain indistinguishable from the standpoint of chains of member and proper part. In view of this, Forrest (2002b), who appears to conceive of proper part in those terms, proposes to make do with a surrogate for the relation a member bears to a class. One advantage of the surrogate in question is that it admits of a purely mereological characterization against the background of Heyting mereology, on which more later. Forrest (2002b) points out how given the existence of a sufficiently rich and varied domain of individuals, one may, in fact, provide surrogates for *pure* classes and mimic the theory of classes. In fact, the framework that results provides a hospitable environment for much of mathematics.

3 The Framework

We have outlined the contours of two rival approaches to the mereology of classes. The purpose of this section is twofold. We will first present a formal framework in which to conduct each investigation, and we will proceed to outline some limitative constraints on each project. We will eventually operate in a plural extension of the language of mereology, which includes a binary relation symbol $\leq$ for *part* as a nonlogical primitive – and $\ll$ as a binary relation symbol for *immediate part* in the case of hierarchical mereology. A plural extension of the language of mereology expands the primitive vocabulary of the language with plural resources, which include plural quantification and plural predication.[23] While the axioms of plural logic are generally common ground to both approaches, they will part ways when it comes to the mereological system they accept.

We proceed in stages. We will first introduce first- and second-order axiomatizations of different mereological systems, and we will later explain how to expand each framework with plural resources. We will take classical logic for granted in what follows, but the reader may consult Cotnoir and Varzi (2021, chapter 6) for the prospects of nonclassical formulations of mereology against the background of alternative logical frameworks.

---

[23] One of the advantages of a plural framework is that it enables us to provide finite axiomatizations of mereology. There are other ways to achieve this by resorting to either quantification over sets or second-order quantification into predicate position. But while second-order formulations of mereology, for example, match the expressive power of plural axiomatizations, they offer a less direct route to the question of whether some objects have a sum or whether they form a class. See Cotnoir and Varzi (2021, chapter 6) for a direct comparison between these approaches.

Mereology

Mereology is the formal theory of the relation of part to whole. It is generally formulated in a first-order language with identity and a nonlogical predicate $\leq$ for part. That is, $x \leq y$ is read: "x is part of y." We define *proper part* and *overlap*, respectively, in terms of part:

$$x < y \quad := \quad x \leq y \wedge x \neq y$$
$$x \circ y \quad := \quad \exists z(z \leq x \wedge z \leq y)$$

So, $x < y$ is read: "x is a proper part of y," which means that x is a part of y other than x. On the other hand, $x \circ y$ is read: "x overlaps y," which means that x and y have some part in common.

To the extent to which we aim to explore different answers to the question of how classes are sums of their proper parts, we should acknowledge that there is more than one formal explication of sum in mereology. Some of them coincide against the background of standard mereological frameworks, but they may well come apart in weaker systems and the difference may become important in what follows. Let us momentarily distinguish three salient candidate explications of sum.[24] The *join* of the instances of a given condition φ is a minimal upper bound of those instances under part, which will be unique given the antisymmetry of part:

$$y = \vee\varphi(x) \quad := \quad \forall x(\varphi(x) \rightarrow x \leq y) \wedge \forall z(\forall x(\varphi(x) \rightarrow x \leq z) \rightarrow y \leq z).$$

In contrast to join, an object y is a *fusion* of the instances of a given condition φ if, and only if, y includes each instance of φ as a part, and every part of y overlaps some instance of φ:

$$Fu_{\varphi(x)}y \quad := \quad \forall x(\varphi(x) \rightarrow x \leq y) \wedge \forall z(z \leq y \rightarrow \exists x(\varphi(x) \wedge z \circ x)).$$

Notice that nothing in the definition of fusion requires fusions to be unique. Indeed, uniqueness is not even a consequence of the assumption that part forms a partial order.

There is finally what Cotnoir and Varzi (2021) call a *Goodman fusion y* of the instances of a given condition φ, which overlaps exactly those objects that overlap some instance of φ: $Fu'_{\varphi(x)}y \quad := \quad \forall z(z \circ y \leftrightarrow \exists x(\varphi(x) \wedge z \circ x)).$

---

[24] They do not, of course, exhaust the range of candidate explanations. See Cotnoir and Varzi (2021, chapter 5) for comparison of a variety of proposals.

Cotnoir and Varzi (2021) compare the three explications of sum and explain how they behave differently in different environments. What is important for present purposes is that they underwrite different standard axiomatizations of mereology.

Classical Extensional Mereology

Classical Extensional Mereology (CEM) emerges as a natural extension of two weaker systems.[25] There is, first, Core Mereology (M), which consists of three partial order axioms:

Reflexivity:	$x \leq x$
Antisymmetry:	$x \leq y \wedge y \leq x \rightarrow x = y$
Transitivity:	$x \leq y \wedge y \leq z \rightarrow x \leq z$

Reflexivity requires objects to be parts of themselves; antisymmetry bars distinct objects from being mutual parts; and transitivity requires the part-to-whole relation to be transitive: if one object is part of a second, and the second part of a third, then the first object is part of the third.

Different axiomatizations of CEM correspond to different extensions of the axioms of core mereology with further axioms concerned with the question of composition and decomposition, respectively. While some axiomatizations are more elegant than others, we want to highlight the range of options available to a theorist who is prepared to relax the axioms of CEM in response to certain conflicts.

The system M makes sure that part is a partial order but remains neutral as to how sums decompose into further parts. We list three candidate axioms in order of strength:

Weak Supplementation:	$x < y \rightarrow \exists z(z \leq y \wedge \neg z \circ x)$
Strong Supplementation:	$x \nleq y \rightarrow \exists z(z \leq x \wedge \neg z \circ y)$
Remainder:	$x \nleq y \rightarrow \exists z \forall u(u \leq z \leftrightarrow (u \leq x \wedge \neg u \circ y))$

Weak supplementation tells us that if a whole has a proper part, then the whole has another part disjoint from the first proper part. If a torso is a proper part of a statue, then the statue has some part with no parts in common with the torso, for example, a head. Strong supplementation is similar: if the statue is not part of the torso, then it has some part with no parts in common with the torso. Finally, remainder requires the existence of a unique maximal part of x which is disjoint from y. This *remainder* may be conceived as the relative complement of y in x, namely, what would remain of x if we deleted y. Neither Weak nor Strong

---

[25] This system receives more than one name in the literature, and it is sometimes called "classical mereology."

Supplementation guarantees the existence of such a remainder on their own, but they do in the presence of appropriate composition principles, on which more in the following discussion.[26]

Minimal (MM) and Extensional Mereology (EM) are the systems that extend Core Mereology with Weak and Strong Supplementation, respectively.

Given the distinction between join, fusion, and Goodman fusion, there is more than one candidate axiom schema for composition. One of them asserts the existence of a join for each *nonempty* condition but leaves open whether the join is a fusion, whereas the other two assert the existence of a fusion for each nonempty condition and one of them explicitly requires the fusion to be unique.

Join:	$\exists x \varphi(x) \rightarrow \exists y \; y = \vee \varphi(x)$
Fusion:	$\exists x \varphi(x) \rightarrow \exists y \; Fu_{\varphi(x)} \; y$
Goodman Fusion:	$\exists x \varphi(x) \rightarrow \exists y \; Fu'_{\varphi(x)} \; y$
Unique Fusion:	$\exists x \varphi(x) \rightarrow \exists ! y \; Fu_{\varphi(x)} y$

There is an array of mereological systems, which supplement the axioms of Core Mereology with different axioms for composition and decomposition, respectively. One of them stands out as a candidate standard for mereology, which is, in fact, CEM.

There are at least four different but equivalent characterizations of CEM:

- Core Mereology + Weak Supplementation + Fusion (Hovda 2009)
- Core Mereology + Strong Supplementation + Goodman Fusion (Eberle 1970; Casati and Varzi 1999)
- Core Mereology + Remainder + Join (Cotnoir and Varzi 2019; Cotnoir and Varzi 2021)
- Transitivity + Unique Fusion (Tarski 1983; Lewis 1991)

What these axiomatizations have in common is that they require part to form a complete Boolean algebra (without the zero element).[27] The distinction between these axiomatizations will eventually be important as they will each suggest different responses to the first limitative constraint we will discuss in the last part of this section.

Classical Extensional Mereology remains neutral with respect to the existence of mereological atoms conceived as objects without a decomposition into proper parts. More precisely, we may tentatively define an object is a mereological *atom* if, and only if, it is not a sum of proper parts. This is equivalent to the claim that the object lacks proper parts against the backdrop

---

[26] See Cotnoir and Varzi (2021, chapter 4) for a comparison of the strength of these supplementation principles.

[27] Cotnoir and Varzi (2021) explain and discuss the result in some detail.

of CEM but not relative to weaker mereological systems introduced in the following discussion.[28] Atomism is often phrased as the thesis that everything has some atom as a part, which, as Cotnoir and Varzi (2019) report, is in the presence of transitivity and strong supplementation, enough to secure the thesis that everything is a fusion of atoms. One salient atomless alternative is to insist that everything is *gunk* understood as something whose parts divide forever into further proper parts.

CEM is the framework David Lewis takes for granted in Lewis (1991) and Lewis (1993). Since the Main Thesis requires singletons to be classes without parts other than themselves, they automatically become mereological atoms.

Heyting Mereology

Hierarchical Composition endows classes with a hierarchical mereological structure: they include members as immediate parts, which may, in turn, come with further immediate parts. On the strict formulation of the hypothesis, there is a distinction between the relation of *immediate part* that a member bears to a class, and the relation of *part* corresponding to the reflexive closure of the ancestral of *immediate part*. On the more liberal formulation of the hypothesis, they include subclasses as further parts. There is a distinction between the relation of *immediate part* that a member bears to a class, and the relation corresponding to the reflexive closure of a hybrid of the relations of member and proper subclass.

As mentioned earlier, one important question is whether to take immediate part as basic and treat part as derivative or whether to take part as a basic and to derive immediate part from it. One reason to prefer the latter option is that immediate part is not transitive: to be an immediate part of an immediate part of a class, for example, is not sufficient in order to be an immediate part of the class. It is not uncommon to think that a nonnegotiable constraint on a basic relation of part is that it should be transitive.[29] There are dissenters, of course, but the case for the transitivity of part seems more robust than the case for other mereological principles.[30]

Heyting mereology provides a framework for a transitive relation of part to whole in line with Hierarchical Composition. This is an extension of Core Mereology that has recently been discussed in connection to this and related

---

[28] We will eventually introduce a contrast between *simples* conceived as objects without proper parts and *atoms* conceived as objects that are not sums of their proper parts.

[29] For explicit articulations of this perspective, consider McDaniel (2009) and Fine (2010). The former requires a relation of part to satisfy a remainder principle, which, as we will soon note, will not be available in Heyting mereology.

[30] See Casati and Varzi (1999) and Cotnoir and Varzi (2019: 3.3) for discussion.

projects, for example, Forrest (2002b), Mormann (2012) and (2013), and Russell (2016). What makes Heyting mereology distinctive is the rejection of many supplementation principles available in classical mereology. One reason to make do without supplementation principles stems from cases of mereological coincidence: to the extent to which a statue and some clay are made of the same matter, something overlaps one if, and only if, it overlaps the other. If we make the further assumption that the clay is a proper part of the statue, we obtain a counterexample to the principle of weak supplementation: The clay is a proper part of the statue, but the clay overlaps everything the statue overlaps. That is the moral Goodman (2022), for example, extracts from the case. Not all friends of coincidence construe the case to be a counterexample to weak supplementation, for example, Cotnoir (2010) presents the case as a counterexample to antisymmetry: the clay and the statue are mutual proper parts.

Hierarchical Composition motivates a much more clear-cut counterexample to weak supplementation. For consider a singleton $\{a\}$ of which a is a proper part according to Hierarchical Composition. Since the parts of $\{a\}$ include a and any parts thereof, every part of $\{a\}$ must overlap a, pace weak supplementation.

Heyting mereology is a salient fallback for subscribers to Hierarchical Composition. One axiomatization of the system results from Cotnoir and Varzi's axiomatization of classical mereology when we replace the axiom of remainder with a complete distributivity axiom, which connects the meet of an object and a join with the join of certain meets. The meet of two objects x and y, which we symbolize $x \wedge y$, is the greatest lower bound under part, which is guaranteed to be unique in the presence of antisymmetry. The complete distributivity axiom now reads:

$$x \wedge \vee \varphi(x) = \vee \exists z (y = (x \wedge z) \wedge \varphi(z)).$$

The models of the system form a Heyting algebra (without a zero element) in which the meet of an object x with a join of the instances of a condition $\varphi(x)$ is the join of the meets of x with each of the instances of $\varphi(x)$. All complete Boolean algebras satisfy the constraint, but not all Heyting algebras are complete Boolean algebras.

To summarize, Heyting mereology is the following system:

• Core Mereology + Complete Distributivity + Join (Forrest 2002b)

We motivated Heyting mereology as a congenial framework for proponents of the hierarchical outlook who remain reluctant to take *immediate part* as basic on the grounds that it is neither reflexive nor transitive. It will now be helpful to highlight some of its distinctive features for present purposes.

One important difference between Heyting and CEM lies in the behavior of the complement operation. Let us define complement in terms of join, as usual:

$$\bar{a} \quad := \quad \vee \neg x \circ a.$$

CEM proves the identity $\bar{\bar{a}} = a$, which may fail in Heyting mereology. To be sure, the system proves that $a \leq \bar{\bar{a}}$, but it leaves open whether $\bar{\bar{a}}$ may include parts, which are themselves not part of a. Given Hierarchical Composition, singletons provide a case in point. Since $a \circ \{a\}$, the complement $\overline{\{a\}}$ of a singleton $\{a\}$ includes neither a nor $\{a\}$ as parts. It follows that the join corresponding to the condition $\neg x \circ \bar{a}$ must, in fact, include $\{a\}$ as a part. Since $\{a\} \not\leq a$, we conclude $\bar{\bar{a}} \not\leq a$. One way to put it is that Heyting mereology is to Classical mereology what intuitionistic logic is to classical logic. Much like intuitionistic logic rejects the equivalence between a proposition and the negation of its negation, Heyting mereology rejects the identification of an object with the complement of its complement. In intuitionistic logic, we may not simply assume that the negation of the negation of a proposition entails that proposition; similarly, in Heyting mereology, we may not simply assume that the complement of the complement of a given object includes that object as a part.

One feature of singletons in this framework is that they are *more than the sum of their proper parts*. For the join of the proper parts of the singleton $\{a\}$ is just a, which is itself a proper part of $\{a\}$. In fact, a is a *maximal proper part* of $\{a\}$, while a proper part of the latter, the former is not a proper part of a proper part of the latter. In line with Simons (1987: 108) and Cotnoir and Varzi (2021, sec. 3.3.2), we may consider a preliminary characterization of immediate part in terms of maximal proper part:

$$x \lhd y := x < y \wedge \neg \exists z (x < z \wedge z < y).$$

Given Hierarchical Composition, each of two individuals a and b would be maximal proper parts of the class $\{a, b\}$: they each would be proper parts of $\{a, b\}$, and none of them would be proper parts of further proper parts of $\{a, b\}$. But whatever its merits, that would still not be the relation of immediate part at play in Hierarchical Composition. For as Fine (1992) observes, we would like to count a as an immediate part of $\{a, \{a\}\}$ even after we acknowledge that it is *not* a maximal proper part of that class. Given Hierarchical Composition, a is a proper part of $\{a\}$, which is, in turn, a proper part of $\{a, \{a\}\}$. Therefore, a is not a maximal proper part of $\{a, \{a\}\}$.

Other relations in the vicinity may approximate the relation of member more closely than that of maximal proper part. One may, for example, take a page from Forrest (2002b) and consider

$xRy := x \lhd y \land \neg \exists z(x \lhd z \land z \lhd y).$

That relation seems closer to immediate part than the relation of maximal proper part. For notice that $\neg aR\{a, \{a\}\}$, since $a \lhd \{a\}$ and $\{a\} \lhd \{\{a\}\}$. One research program in the area becomes to investigate the question of whether such a relation provides us with a mathematically fruitful surrogate for the member relation.

Forrest (2002b) embarks in a similar project. One difference is that his point of departure is closer to Liberal Hierarchical Composition, which means that the first pass at a preliminary characterization of member is the relation of maximal proper part of a part:

$x \trianglelefteq y := \exists z(x \lhd z \land z \leq y).$

Given Liberal Hierarchical Composition, two individuals a and b would be maximal proper parts of parts of the class $\{a, b\}$: they each would be maximal proper parts of $\{a\}$ and $\{b\}$, respectively, which are themselves proper parts of $\{a, b\}$. But notice that a is, in fact, a maximal proper part of a part of $\{\{a\}\}$, that is, a is a maximal proper part of $\{a\}$, which is part of $\{\{a\}\}$, even though a is not a member of $\{\{a\}\}$.

One reaction to this is to attempt to make do with another surrogate for the relation of member:

$xEy := x \trianglelefteq y \land \neg \exists z(x \trianglelefteq z \land z \trianglelefteq y).$

Indeed, Forrest (2002b) observes that this relation is in fact mathematically fruitful and supports a framework within which to interpret much of pure set theory against the background of the existence of a sufficiently rich and varied domain of individuals.

Hierarchical Mereology

We described Heyting mereology as a theory of the relation of part to whole within which to mimic a relation of immediate part. The fact that the system does not support a faithful characterization of immediate part in terms of part suggests a different tack. That is to seek an axiomatization of hierarchical mereology as a theory of immediate part within which to characterize part as a derived mereological relation. The plan now, that is, is to take the relation of immediate part as basic and to characterize part in terms of it. That will allow us to do justice to the hierarchical mereological structure of complex objects as formed out of some immediate parts as they are bound by a relation or a principle of unity.[31]

---

[31] One inspiration for these views is Aristotle's *hylomorphic* conception of complex material objects as composed of matter unified by a certain form. Fine (1999), Johnston (2006), and Koslicki (2008) articulate contemporary variations on the same theme.

What is perhaps the most developed framework for hierarchical mereology comes from Fine (1999). Fine originally operates in an interpreted first-order language with predicates of different adicities and a primitive predicate $\leq$ for *part*. Fortunately, as Jacinto and Cotnoir (2019) observe, it is not difficult to reformulate the theory with a primitive predicate for *immediate part* for which we use the symbol $\ll$.[32] The operation of rigid embodiment combines certain objects into a mereological complex, which Fine calls a *rigid embodiment* whose immediate parts stand in certain relations to each other.

The informal core of the theory of rigid embodiments is this. Given some objects $a, b, c, \ldots$ related by a relation R, there is a *rigid embodiment* $a, b, c, \ldots / R$ composed of $a, b, c, \ldots$ and R. The objects $a, b, c, \ldots$ and the relation R are its *immediate parts*. The objects $a, b, c, \ldots$ are *material parts* of the embodiment, and R is the principle of embodiment.

A water molecule would be a paradigmatic example of a rigid embodiment, which consists of two hydrogen atoms linked with an oxygen atom by certain covalent bonds. The two hydrogen atoms and the oxygen atom are its material parts, and the link between them is its principle of embodiment.

Fine (1999) lays down six postulates for rigid embodiments. Two specify their existence and identity conditions, one governs their interaction with location, and three more postulates govern their interaction with the relation of part to whole. Here is a reformulation of the postulates in terms of immediate part.

R1. (Existence): $a, b, c, \ldots / R$ exists at w if, and only if, R relates $a, b, c \ldots$ at w.

R2. (Location): If $a, b, c, \ldots / R$ exists at w, then $a, b, c, \ldots / R$ is located at a point p in w if, and only if, at least one of $a, b, c \ldots$ is located at p in w.

R3. (Identity): $a, b, c, \ldots / R = a', b', c', \ldots / R'$ if, and only if, $a = a'$, $b = b'$, $c = c', \ldots$, and $R = R'$.

R4. (Material Immediate Part): Each of $a, b, c, \ldots$ are immediate parts of $a, b, c, \ldots / R$. They each are a *material* immediate part of the embodiment.

R5. (Formal Immediate Part): R is an immediate part of $a, b, c \ldots / R$. The relation is a *formal* immediate part of the embodiment.

We may now characterize the relation of part as the reflexive closure of the ancestral of immediate part: x is part of y if, and only if, x is an ancestral immediate part of y or $x = y$.

---

[32] They provide an independent argument for the indefinability of immediate part in terms of part in the system and characterize part as the reflexive closure of the ancestral of immediate part.

One further constraint makes sure that a rigid embodiment has no parts that are not themselves parts of either its immediate material parts or its principle of embodiment.

R6. A part of $a, b, c, \ldots$ is a part of one of $a, b, c, \ldots$ or a part of R.

Some clarification is in order. Notice first that postulates R2 and R5 will play a minimal role in what follows. The purpose of R2 is to secure appropriate locations for rigid embodiments, which are inherited from its immediate parts. Postulate R5 gives expression to the thought that the form that unifies certain objects into an embodiment is itself an immediate part of the embodiment. While that may strike some as an attractive thought, it is not universally accepted by subscribers to hierarchical perspective, for example, Johnston (2006). More importantly for our purposes, it seems to be in conflict with the letter of Hierarchical Composition.

The existence and identity postulates should presumably be understood against the background of an independent theory of relations, which constraints the interpretation of the predicates of the language. They are, for example, sensitive to the individuation conditions for relations. To use Fine's own example, suppose you make a distinction between the relation one object bears to another when the first is placed *above* the second and the relation one bears to another when the second is placed *below* the first. That would impose very fine-grained identity conditions for rigid embodiments: the rigid embodiment whose members are a and b when a is above b would be different from the rigid embodiment whose members are a and b when b is below a.[33] There is a similar question for the combination of existence and identity, which may be thought to collapse into an inconsistent principle on a theory of relations on which no matter what objects may be, there are related by at least one relation.[34] Indeed, Fairchild (2017) raises a similar difficulty for the assumption that no matter what an object may be, for every property F the object exemplifies, there is a rigid embodiment of the form a/F.

The theory of rigid embodiments is supplemented with an account of variable embodiments. The core of the theory of variable embodiments is this. Given an individual concept F, there is a *variable embodiment* $/F/$, which is manifested by whatever objects are F at different times. Fine takes a car to be a prototypical example of a variable embodiment, one which is at a given time manifested by

---

[33] Fine explains how to obtain more coarse-grained identity conditions if one reformulates the identity postulate in terms of states of affairs: $a, b, c, \ldots /R = a', b', c', \ldots /R'$ if, and only if, the state of affairs, which consists of $a, b, c, \ldots$ standing in R is the same as the state of affairs, which consists of $a', b', c', \ldots$ standing in R'.

[34] We will discuss this limitation in what follows.

a rigid embodiment whose immediate members are different car parts such as the chasis, the engine, the wheel, and so on, and whose form is a certain relation in which the different immediate parts stand to each other. He later gives a series of postulates for variable embodiments, which would take us too far afield from our focus. Since hierarchical composition invites the identification of classes of rigid embodiments of a certain sort, and variable embodiments will play no role in the implementation of the proposal.

In order to formulate a perfectly general theory of embodiments, we ascend to a second-order language with a binary relation symbol $\ll$ for immediate part and a range of second-order variables X^n of the same syntactic category as n-place predicates. The ascent to a second-order language is part of what will allow us to offer an explicit definition of part in terms of immediate part in line with Jacinto and Cotnoir (2019: 933):

$$x \leq y := \quad \forall X((\forall u(x \ll u \rightarrow Xu) \land \forall u \forall t((Xu \land u \ll t \rightarrow Xt)) \rightarrow Xy) \lor x = y \cdot$$

That is, x is part of y if, and only if, x stands in the ancestral of immediate part to y or $x = y$. Or, equivalently, x stands in the weak ancestral of immediate part to y.

We now regiment the rest of the principles in line with Jacinto and Cotnoir (2019). We use $\vec{x}_n$ as abbreviations for finite sequences of variables $x_1, \ldots, x_n$.[35] We have omitted the initial quantifiers in order to enhance readability, but notice that we have the resources to express each axiom as a universal generalization.

$R1 \quad \exists x \, x = \vec{y}_n / R^n \leftrightarrow R^n \vec{y}_n$

$R3 \quad \exists x \, x = \vec{y}_n / R^n \rightarrow (\vec{x}_n / R^n = \vec{y}_m / S^m \leftrightarrow (\bigwedge_{1 \leq i \leq m} x_i = y_i \land R^n = S^m))$

$R4 \quad \exists x \, x = \vec{y}_n / R^n \rightarrow \bigwedge_{1 \leq i \leq m} x_i \ll \vec{x}_n / R^n$

$R5 \quad \exists x \, x = \vec{y}_n / R^n \rightarrow R^n \ll \vec{x}_n / R^n$

$R6 \quad (x \leq \vec{y}_n / R^n \rightarrow \bigvee_{1 \leq i \leq m} x \leq y_i) \land (S \leq \vec{y}_n / R^n \rightarrow \bigvee_{1 \leq i \leq m} S^m \leq y_i \lor S^m R^n)$

This provides a candidate framework for an articulation of Hierarchical Composition similar to the one Caplan, Tillman, and Reeder (2010) undertake.[36] One apparent limitation of the provisional framework we have outlined is that we have by default restricted attention to rigid embodiments composed of finitely many immediate parts as they exemplify a finitary relation,

---

[35] They qualify the antecedent of R3, R4, and R5 to take into account the fact that a rigid embodiment may not exist at a time at which its immediate parts exist but they are not appropriately related in accordance to the principle of embodiment.

[36] We have omitted the formulation of R2, which is not directly relevant to the present project.

and one may want to allow for a more liberal form of existence for rigid embodiments. The resources of plural logic will eventually allow us to do just that.

We have considered first-order formulations of each mereological framework, but they receive a more perspicuous formulation against the background of a plural extension of the language.

Plural Logic

Given a first-order language L, we consider the plural expansion that results when we extend its vocabulary with a range of plural variables xx, yy, zz with or without subscripts and a binary predicate $x \prec xx$ with a singular and a plural argument. That marks a crucial difference with respect to binary predicates flanked by singular arguments such as $x \leq y$ or $x \in y$. The plural variables are formal counterparts of natural language plural pronouns such as 'they' and 'them' and they are bound by a plural quantifier as in formulas of the form $\forall xx \varphi$ or $\exists xx \varphi$. Atomic formulas of the form $x \prec xx$ are read: "x is one of xx".

What makes plural quantification distinctive is that it is in principle irreducible to covert singular quantification over the domain. The plural expansion of the language of set theory contains the formula

$$\exists xx \forall x (x \prec xx \leftrightarrow x \notin x),$$

which tells us that there are some sets such that a set is one of them if, and only if, it is non–self-membered. But notice that to claim that some sets are all and only non–self-membered sets is *not* to claim that some *setlike* object contains all and only non–self-membered sets. For only the first claim is true when we quantify over the domain of sets and exclude setlike objects that are not sets. This is indeed how George Boolos motivated the distinctive feature of plural quantification in Boolos (1984) and Boolos (1985).

Let us pause for a terminological aside. Even if we take to heart the point that plural quantification is not covert singular quantification over the domain, we will sometimes and for ease of communication speak in the singular of a plurality of such and such objects. While such talk is grammatically singular, it is officially eliminated in terms of plural reference to the such and such objects.

We read atomic formulas of the form $x \prec xx$ as: "x is one of xx", and we use $\prec$ to define two more relation symbols flanked by plural terms:

$$xx \preccurlyeq yy \quad := \quad \forall z (z \prec xx \rightarrow z \prec yy)$$
$$xx \approx yy \quad := \quad xx \preccurlyeq yy \wedge yy \preccurlyeq xx$$

$xx \preccurlyeq yy$ is read: "xx are among yy", and $xx \approx yy$ is read: "xx are the same as yy"

One more clarification. The plural quantifier $\exists xx$ is read as "there are some objects xx," but this in turn is interpreted differently by different authors. Some take it to mean that there are two or more objects xx, whereas it is more common to understand it to mean that there is one or more objects xx. Still others interpret it to mean that there are zero or more objects xx. In what follows, we will take it to mean that there is one or more objects. Florio and Linnebo (2021) codify the commitment by means of an axiom:

$$\forall xx \, \exists y \, y \prec xx.$$

We are now in a position to provide plural formulations of axioms of join and fusion in the expanded plural language. We define the join of some objects xx as their minimal upper bound under part, which, given antisymmetry, is unique if it exists. Likewise, we declare an object y to be a fusion of some objects xx if y includes everything in xx as a part and includes only parts that overlap with them.

$$y = \vee xx \quad := \quad \forall x(x \prec xx \rightarrow x \leq y) \wedge \forall z(\forall x(x \prec xx \rightarrow x \leq z) \rightarrow y \leq z)$$
$$F(xx, y) \quad := \quad \forall x(x \prec xx \rightarrow x \leq y) \wedge \forall z(z \leq y \rightarrow \exists x(x \prec xx \wedge y \circ x))$$

There are plural forms of the axioms of join and fusion, respectively, but their content is sensitive to the range of plural variables to range. In order to at least match the expressive power of the first-order schema, we should make sure that no matter what condition $\varphi(x)$ framed in the language of mereology may be, some objects are exactly those which satisfy the condition $\varphi(x)$.

Plural logic generally includes an axiom of plural comprehension according to which there are, for each nonvacuous condition $\varphi(x)$, where x occurs free, some objects, which are exactly those objects that satisfy the condition:

$$\exists x\varphi(x) \rightarrow \exists xx \forall x(x \prec xx \leftrightarrow \varphi(x)) \qquad \text{Plural Comprehension}$$

In the plural expansion of the language of set theory, given the condition $x \notin x$, which is not vacuous, plural comprehension delivers the existence of some objects, which are exactly the non–self-membered objects:

$$\exists x\varphi(x) \rightarrow \exists xx \forall x(x \prec xx \leftrightarrow x \notin x).$$

The axiom schema of plural comprehension is generally combined with another axiom schema of plural indiscernibility, which encodes the presupposition that plurals are extensional. That is, whatever is true of some objects remains true of some other objects if they are coextensive with the former:

$$xx \approx yy \rightarrow (\Phi(xx) \leftrightarrow \Phi(yy)) \qquad \text{Plural Indiscernibility}$$

This axiom is *almost* universally accepted and embodies the thought that plurals are extensional.[37]

What is perhaps the fundamental theorem of plural logic gives voice to the Cantorian fact that there are strictly more pluralities than objects. But it takes some effort to even make sense of that claim in a plural language. We have been adamant that talk of pluralities is to be officially eliminated in favor of plural talk, but it is not obvious how to do that in this case. In order to properly frame the plural generalization of Cantor's theorem, we must explain how to make sense of cardinality comparisons between the range of plural variables and that of singular variables. Since pluralities are not objects, we are not in a position to explain such comparisons in terms of the existence or nonexistence of a map from the range of plural variables to the range of singular variables. For that would require one to move beyond the expressive resources of the plural expansion of a first-order language.

Instead, following Shapiro (1991: 104), we quantify over binary relations over the domain in order to simulate such maps. If R is a binary relation, we extract a map from the plural into the singular domain as follows: R maps xx into x if and only if they are all and only objects in the domain of R, which the relation pairs with x. We can now make sense of an injection of the range of plural variables into that of singular variables in terms of the existence of a binary relation R such that

$$\forall xx\, \exists x \forall y\, (Ryx \leftrightarrow y \prec xx).$$

Such a relation may relate the members of a given plurality to more than one object, but notice that if such a relation existed, then we would be in a position to inject pluralities into objects.

Alas, there is a plural generalization of Cantor's theorem:

Proposition 3.1 $\exists x \exists y\, x \neq y \rightarrow \neg \forall xx\, \exists x \forall y (Rxy \leftrightarrow y \prec xx)$

In other words, if there is more than one object, then no binary relation will be able to encode an injective map from the range of plural variables into the domain.

Proof Outline Suppose a binary relation R encodes an injective map from the range of plural variables into the domain. Plural Comprehension now delivers:

$$\exists x \neg Rxx \rightarrow \exists xx \forall x (x \prec xx \leftrightarrow \neg Rxx).$$

---

[37] One exception is Uzquiano (2018), which generalizes plural talk to make allowance for coextensive plural embodiments to remain distinct on the grounds that they have a distinct modal profile.

Since there is more than one object, the condition $\neg Rxx$ is not vacuous, which means:

$$\exists xx \forall x (x \prec xx \leftrightarrow \neg Rxx).$$

Let rr be such objects and let r be the object into which R maps rr:

$$\forall y (Rry \leftrightarrow y \prec yy).$$

Universal instantiation now gives us

$$Rrr \leftrightarrow \neg Rrr,$$

whence a contradiction follows.

One immediate consequence of the theorem is the inconsistency – modulo the existence of more than one object – of the principle that no matter what some objects may be, there is a set of them, which Florio and Linnebo (2021) have recently discussed:

$$\forall xx \exists x \forall y (y \in x \leftrightarrow y \prec xx).$$

The problem arises when we interpret Rxy in terms of $\in$, and the standard approach to this observation is to regard it as a limitative constraint on the interaction of plural logic and set theory. What is distinctive of the outlook Florio and Linnebo (2021) advocate is precisely to reverse the situation and fault the uncritical adherence to instances of plural comprehension for the inconsistency. They argue instead that plural logic should indeed be able to accommodate Plural Collapse at the cost of Plural Comprehension. Critical Plural Logic does not underwrite the instances of comprehension we used in order to derive the plural formulation of Cantor's theorem, and it provides yet another fallback that is immune to the limitative constraints of the next section.

Limitative Constraints

We will now operate within a plural mereological framework. David Lewis, for example, articulated his defense of the Main Thesis against the background of a plural formulation of CEM, and we will frame part of the discussion of Hierarchical Composition against the background of a plural formulation of the theory of rigid embodiments. Each approach, however, is subject to important limitative constraints that are closely related to the fundamental theorem of plural logic.

Classical Extensional Mereology

One important difference between pluralities and fusions is that fusions need not come with a unique decomposition into parts: a fusion of statues is a fusion of torsos, heads, and limbs as much as it is a fusion of statues even if most of those parts are not themselves statues. Matters are different for pluralities, since a plurality of statues consists exclusively of statues and not of torsos, heads, or limbs. In this respect, pluralities behave less like fusions and more like classes.

On occasion, we are able to use fusions to mimic the behavior of classes. Lewis (1970) observed that in favorable circumstances, if we use a condition θ to distinguish some parts of a fusion, we may find that the fusion comes with a unique decomposition into θ-parts. Fusions of θ-parts behave much like pluralities of θ-objects, and the relation a θ-part bears to a fusion of θ-parts is perfectly parallel to the relation a θ-object bears to a plurality of θ-objects. For ease of exposition, we will write that a condition θ is a *filter* if, and only if, a fusion of θ-parts has a unique decomposition into θ-parts.

The condition $\forall y(y \leq x \rightarrow x \leq y)$, which corresponds to *atomicity*, is a filter. The fusion of some atoms has a unique decomposition into atoms.[38] This is because no atom is part of another atom, and no atom is part of a fusion of atoms that do not include it. More generally, since no two atoms overlap, given the definition of fusion, a fusion of some atoms is one and the same as a fusion of others if, and only if, each of the former is one of the latter and vice versa.

Lewis (1970) noticed that when the language is expanded to formulate the condition of being a maximal spatiotemporal connected object, we find that maximal spatiotemporal connected parts behaved much like classes of maximal spatiotemporal connected objects and used this observation to explain how to exploit it to mimic the behavior of classes in a purely mereological framework. One limitation of the method is that there is no reason whatever to think that all objects are in fact θ-objects, whether mereological atoms or maximal spatio-temporal connected parts or what have you.

One may hope to do better if one is able to find a θ-code for each and every object. That is, one would do better if one could a θ-code to each object and treat fusions of θ-parts as surrogates for classes of the objects they encode. That is, in fact, part and parcel of the approach Lewis takes in Lewis (1991) where the language of mereology is expanded to include a singleton operation. Since, for Lewis, singletons are atoms, a fusion of singletons has a unique decomposition into singletons and the relation an object bears to a fusion of singletons if its singleton is part of it is akin to the member relation. The singleton operation provides a code for each object, which allows us to use fusions of such codes to play the role of classes.

---

[38] CEM makes sure the fusion is unique.

There is a limitative result closely related to plural Cantor. Given a *filter* θ, we write that ρ is a total θ-coding if, and only if, ρ is an operation that satisfies three conditions:

Totality : $\exists y\, y = \rho(x)$
Injectivity : $\rho(x) = \rho(y) \to x = y$
θ-coding : $\theta(\rho(x))$

Totality makes sure that ρ provides a code for each object, whereas Injectivity ensures that different objects are assigned different codes. The third, and last condition, requires that the codes be θ-objects. We are now in a position to state the first limitative result:

Proposition 3.2 Given a filter θ, CEM is, modulo the existence of more than one object, inconsistent with the existence of a total θ-coding.

Proof Outline If θ is a filter, then a total θ-coding would enable us to define a binary relation R for which

$$\forall xx\, \exists x \forall y (Rxy \leftrightarrow y \prec xx).$$

Given some objects xx, we would let x be the fusion of their θ-codes, and we would define:

$$Rxy := \rho(y) \leq x.$$

If $y \leq xx$, the $\rho(y)$, which is a θ-code for y would be a θ-part of x, which is the fusion of θ-codes of each of xx. On the other hand, if y is a θ-part of x, which is the fusion of θ-codes of each of xx, then given the fact that θ is a filter, we would have that y is one of xx.

The existence of such a binary relation is now in direct conflict with Cantor's theorem for plural logic.

One corollary of this observation is the observation Gideon Rosen made in Rosen (1995), and recently rehearsed in McCarthy (2015), where $\theta(u)$ is $\forall x(x \leq u \to x = u)$, that is, u is a mereological atom. One immediate consequence of the Main Thesis is that singletons are atoms, which means that as a corollary, we find that if the Main Thesis is true, then there is no total coding of objects by singletons. The problem is more general, and it generalizes to other approaches on which being a singleton is in fact a filter. We do not evade the difficulty if we simply reject atomicity on the grounds, for example, that all singletons share a common part in line with the suggestions Armstrong (1991) and Caplan, Tillman, and Reeder (2010) make. The former suggest that singletons include the null set as a further part, whereas the latter suggests that singletons have parts other than classes. But the threat of inconsistency persists provided that we maintain that the condition of being a singleton is a filter and a fusion of singletons continues to have a unique decomposition into singletons.[39]

Hierarchical Mereology

We now look at a plural variation on the theory of rigid embodiments introduced earlier. We expand a first-order language with a primitive predicate $\ll$ for *immediate part* into a plural language supplemented with a stock of plural predicates $P, Q, \ldots$ with a plural argument. These plural predicates express attributes some objects may exemplify. One may now reformulate *some* of Fine's postulates in the enriched plural language. The plural formulation of the existence postulate posits a rigid embodiment whenever some objects xx exemplify some attribute X:

PR1. (Plural Existence): xx/P exists at w if, and only if, Pxx at w.

PR2. (Location): If xx/P exists at w, then xx/P is located at a point p in w if, and only if, at least one of xx is located at p in w.

PR3. (Plural Identity): $xx/P = yy/Q$ if, and only if, $xx \approx yy$, and $P = Q$.

This last postulate is, of course, sensitive to what we take to be the identity conditions for attributes. One option is to deem P and Q to be identical if they are necessarily coextensive in a suitably expanded language with a modal operator $\Box$ for metaphysical necessity:

$$\Box \forall xx(Pxx \leftrightarrow Qxx) \rightarrow P = Q.$$

More fine-grained views of the identity conditions for attributes would require yet a different interpretation of the postulate, but the difference is not important for present purposes.

The next principle specifies the immediate parts of a rigid embodiment:

PR4. (Immediate Part): Each of xx are immediate parts of xx/P.

We do not offer a plural formulation of the fifth postulate because nothing in the letter of Hierarchical Composition requires a plural attribute P to be an immediate part of the rigid embodiment xx/P.

We continue to understand part as the weak ancestral of part, which will now be couched in plural terms. Armed with a definition of part in terms of proper part, we formulate one final constraint on the natura of rigid embodiments

---

[39] Caplan, Tillman, and Reeder (2010) do not subscribe to classical mereology, and they do not identify a class with a fusion of singletons but rather a rigid embodiment of its members as they exemplify some attribute.

according to which the parts of the immediate parts of a rigid embodiment exhaust the range of its parts:

PR6. (Part) A part of xx/P is a part of one of xx.

Here is the official definition of part in terms of immediate part:

$$x \leq y := \quad \forall xx((\forall u(x \ll u \rightarrow u \prec xx) \land$$
$$\forall u \forall t \big((u \prec xx \land u \ll t \rightarrow t \prec xx)\big) \rightarrow y \prec xx) \lor x = y$$

What follows is the plural formulation of the four postulates we adopt as part of our official formulation of hierarchical mereology:

PR1　　$\exists x\ x = xx/P \leftrightarrow Pxx$
PR3　　$\exists x\ x = xx/P \rightarrow (xx/P = yy/Q \leftrightarrow xx \approx yy \land P = Q)$
PR4　　$\exists x\ x = xx/P \rightarrow \forall x(x \prec xx \rightarrow x \ll xx/P)$
PR6　　$x \leq xx/P \rightarrow \exists y(y \prec xx \land x \leq y)$

The combination of the existence and identity postulates now places us on the brink of inconsistency on abundantist views of attributes. For let E be a plural attribute some objects exemplify just in case each of them exists:

$\Box\ (Exx \leftrightarrow \forall x(x \prec xx \rightarrow \exists y\ x = y))$.

No matter what some objects may be, such a plural attribute will bind them into a rigid embodiment xx/E, which, given PR1, exists whenever the objects in question exist. But given PR2, unless some objects xx coincide with some objects yy, the rigid embodiments xx/E and yy/E, respectively, will differ from each other, $xx/E \neq yy/E$.

Proposition 3.3 The plural formulation of the existence and identity postulates is inconsistent with the existence of more than one object.

Proof Outline The plural formulation of the existence and identity postulates enable us to define a binary relation R for which

$\forall xx\ \exists x \forall y(Rxy \leftrightarrow y \prec xx)$.

For let E be the attribute some objects exemplify just in case they each exist. Define:

$Rxy := \exists xx(y = xx/E \land x \ll y)$.

On the one hand, given the plural identity postulate, the immediate parts of a rigid embodiment of the form xx/E are exactly the objects x such that $x \prec xx$. On the other hand, given some objects xx, they will trivially satisfy the condition $xx \preccurlyeq xx$, which means that there is, according to the plural identity postulate, a rigid embodiment xx/E, which consist of those objects to the extent to which they satisfy the condition.

The existence of such a relation would now be in direct conflict with Cantor's theorem for plural logic.

This is in line with the observation Caplan, Tillman, and Reeder (2010) make on p. 45. They propose instead to replace the plural existence postulate with one on which rigid embodiments are formed in stages of a cumulative hierarchy. There is first a level of individuals without immediate parts. At the next level, we find rigid embodiments of individuals bound by different attributes. At the next level, we find rigid embodiments of individuals and/or rigid embodiments found at some earlier level bound by different attributes, and so on. For a more compact formulation of the thesis, we write that rigid embodiments are formed in stages. Given some rigid embodiments and/or individuals found at some stage, there is a rigid embodiment whose immediate parts are exactly those objects as they exemplify a given attribute.

4 The Main Thesis

The time has come to refine the two broad approaches to the mereology of classes we outlined at the outset. One stance identifies the parts of a class with its subclasses, whereas the other endows classes with a hierarchical mereological structure: their parts include their members, the members of its members, and so forth. We will now explain some of the choice points each proposal faces and we will discuss the prospects of a fruitful implementation of each stance. We devote this chapter to implementations of the first approach of which Lewis (1991) and Lewis (1993) are prime instances. One important contrast, for Lewis, is that between classes, which have members, and individuals, which do not. Lewis proceeds to classify the empty set as an individual rather than a class, but the decision is meant to be inconsequential; his suggestion is just to choose one individual to play the role of the empty set. That means that the Main Thesis remains largely silent when it comes to the mereological structure of the empty set – except for the fact that it is neither part of a class nor does it include a class as a part. The concern of the Main Thesis is the mereological structure of classes, which are exactly those objects that have members. We now look at the question of how to motivate the Main Thesis.

Motivation

In Lewis (1991) and Lewis (1993), David Lewis derives the Main Thesis from two other theses:

The First Thesis One class is part of another if, and only if, the first is a subclass of the second.[40]

---
[40] See Lewis (1991, 4).

The First Thesis is supposed to derive support from a variety of consider-ations. We mentioned at the outset that it accords well with certain aspects of common usage: we use the word 'part' to refer to the relation a subclass bears to a class, for example, the class of axioms is part of the class of theorems of a system. But these considerations have limited purchase, especially when they are set against other aspects of common speech: we often describe classes as composed of their members, which would suggest their members are further parts of the class. That, however, would be counter to the First Thesis given that not all members of a class are subclasses of it. So, subscribers to the First Thesis must dismiss such talk as nonliteral or as a figure of speech.

One common source of support for the First Thesis is the observation that much like part, the subclass relation is a partial ordering of classes, one that satisfies strong supplementation and fusion at least against the background of certain theories of classes. Furthermore, much like mereological fusions, clas-ses submit to more than one decomposition into subclasses. The formal analogy between part and subclass is meant as just another piece of evidence, albeit inconclusive, for the identification between subclass and the relation of part to whole on the domain of classes.

The First Thesis leaves open whether a class may include objects other than its subclasses as further parts, for example, individuals such as the null set or fusions of individuals and classes. This is exactly the question that the Second Thesis is supposed to settle:

The Second Thesis No class has any part that is not a class.[41]

The parts of a class are *exclusively* its subclasses. Against the background of classical mereology, Lewis derives the Second Thesis from the First Thesis in combination with three other theses:

The Division Thesis Everything is an individual, a class, or a fusion thereof.

The Priority Thesis No class is part of an individual.

The Fusion Thesis A fusion of individuals is an individual.

For Lewis, the Priority Thesis and the Fusion Thesis are meant to capture the thought that individuals are prior to classes. We may not know yet how individuals will figure in the construction of classes, but we know that they themselves are composed of further individuals.

The argument proceeds by reductio. For the Second Thesis to fail, there would have to be a class X, which includes a nonclass as a part. Given the

---
[41] See Lewis (1991, 6).

Division Thesis, the nonclass in question must be either an individual or a mixed fusion of individuals and classes. Either way, X must include an individual as a part. Consider the fusion u of individuals that are parts of X, which, by the Fusion Thesis, must itself be an individual. By remainder, we may consider their mereological difference $X \backslash u$, which is the fusion of parts of X that are not parts of u. Since $X \backslash U$ has no individuals as parts, it must, by the Division Thesis, be a class. It follows that the original class X is, in fact, a fusion of a class $X \backslash u$ and an individual u. The First Thesis tells us that since $X \backslash u$ is a part of X, it is one of its subclasses. But being a *proper* subclass of X, it must fail to contain a member A of $X \backslash u$. Let $\{A\}$ be the singleton of A. By the First Thesis, $\{A\}$ is part of X but not part of $X \backslash u$; moreover, by the Priority Thesis, $\{A\}$ is not part of u. So, by strong supplementation, $\{A\}$ has a proper part B that does not overlap u. No individual is part of B, which means that B is a class by the Division Thesis. By the First Thesis, B is a proper subclass of $\{A\}$, which is inconsistent with the fact that singletons have no proper subclasses.

It is important to highlight the role of CEM in the argument. Even if Lewis' opponents are prepared to acknowledge a derivative sense in which subclasses are parts of classes, they might remain unmoved by the use of strong supplementation in the subsequent argument. It is true that the combination of the First Thesis with the three subordinate theses entails the Second Thesis against the background of CEM, but at the end of the day, it is better to acknowledge that the best case for the Second Thesis is that it ultimately leads to an attractive and powerful theory of classes.

Another consideration may, however, be brought to bear on the question of whether a class has parts other than its subclasses. One may argue that singletons have no proper parts on the grounds that if they do, they should include their sole member. But that would be in tension with the view that a doubleton $\{a, b\}$ is a fusion of two singletons $\{a\}$ and $\{b\}$. The problem is this: if singletons include their members as a proper part, then $a < \{a\} < \{\{a\}\}$, which means that $\{\{a\}\}$ is the join of $\{a\}$ and $\{\{a\}\}$. Therefore, $\{\{a\}\} = \{a, \{a\}\}$ and $a = \{a\}$, which is generally not true. The argument just now outlined made no use of supplementation principles, just the assumption that a singleton has its sole member as a part and the stipulation that a doubleton is the join of the singletons of its members.

One apparent advantage of the Main Thesis is that it helps alleviate the mystery of classes by subsuming them under the category of fusions, which, for Lewis at least, is unproblematic and perfectly understood. Classes, unfortunately, are fusions of *singletons*, which are less well understood. The Main Thesis tells us that a class has a decomposition into singletons, which are mereologically simple. To the extent to which they lack further internal mereological structure, they remain a black box from a strictly mereological standpoint, which means that we have no means to recover their members from their mereological structure alone.

The Main Thesis reduces the mystery of classes to the mystery of singletons, which Lewis seems to find insurmountable. It follows from the Second Thesis that the sole member of a singleton class is not part of it, which means that there is a nonmereological link between the sole member of a singleton and the singleton. He claims we know nothing when it comes to the nature of singletons or that of the nonmereological relation between it and its sole member. Oliver and Smiley (2006) and Oliver and Smiley (2018) take an even bleaker view of singletons and prefer to confront the original mystery.[42] Since singletons are classes, given the Main Thesis, they have no parts other than themselves, and are therefore mereological atoms. This makes the nonmereological relation an object bears to its singleton all the more mysterious.

The burden of the nonmereological link between an object and its singleton becomes more tolerable when set against the range of benefits they afford. We know from Proposition 2.1 that given the Main Thesis, there is *no* strictly mereological definition of member in terms of part. The situation changes in the presence of a singleton operation, which allows us to define *member* in terms of the nonmereological link between an object and its *singleton* and *part*: to be a member of a class is to have a singleton that is a part of the class. To the extent to which the nonmereological link between an object and its singleton is required in order to make sense of *member*, which is the central concept of set theory, Lewis thinks we have no choice but to accept it. Set theory – and the rest of mathematics – rests on firmer ground than the epistemological concerns we may raise against them.

One way to retain the benefits of singletons without the epistemological baggage they carry with them is to opt for a structuralist approach to the singleton operation. No knowledge of the nature of singletons is required in order to acknowledge that a singleton operation must satisfy a variety of structural conditions set forth in the axioms of set theory. The structuralist account of singleton allows us to reduce the theory of classes to the combination of classical mereology and a general theory of singleton.

Other philosophers are more sanguine when it comes to the prospects of an intelligible account of the singleton operation and the nonmereological link between an object and its singleton. Largely moved by Lewis' epistemological concerns, they are reluctant to take the singleton operation at face value as a special instance of a mathematical *set of* operation, which, according to Gödel

---

[42] Kanamori (2003) discusses the history of singletons in set theory.

(1947) for example, constitutes the subject matter of set theory. While not all of them subscribe to the Main Thesis, their proposals could nonetheless be combined with it. David Armstrong identifies singletons with certain states of affairs in Armstrong (1991) and John Bigelow identifies them with haecceities in Bigelow (1993).[43] Other candidates are not difficult to isolate: self-identity tropes in the manner of D. C. Williams, tropes (Forrest 2002a), and rigid embodiments (Caplan, Tillman, and Reeder 2010).[44]

What these approaches have in common is that they require caution when combined with the Main Thesis. For singletons are categorized as mereological atoms according to the Main Thesis, which means that they form a filter. To the extent to which the singleton operation provides a total coding of objects into fusions of atoms, we find ourselves in direct conflict with Proposition 3.2, which is the first limitative result we recorded in the previous section.

A Dilemma

David Lewis takes both CEM and the Main Thesis as unproblematic and well-understood, but one faces a dilemma when combining them with a theory of the singleton operation. For the Main Thesis entails that singletons are atoms, and a total injection of objects into singletons is, modulo the existence of more than one object, inconsistent with CEM.[45] Since the Main Thesis is nonnegotiable for present purposes, we face a dilemma. We should either restrict the scope of the singleton operation or else we should be prepared to weaken CEM. The first option fits well with the structuralist approach to singletons David Lewis embraces in Lewis (1991) and Lewis (1993), whereas the outlook of Armstrong (1991) and Forrest (2002a) fits better with the second option. They both opt for a reduction of the singleton operation to one they take to be better understood, but it is in each case difficult to motivate a restriction in the scope of the operation they choose for the reduction.[46]

Our formulation of the dilemma sets aside more radical responses to the problem such as a fallback to *critical* plural logic or even to weaker nonclassical

---

[43] However, Bigelow departs from the Main Thesis to the extent to which he proceeds to identify sets with plural haecceities as opposed to sums of singular haecceities. The point remains that a proponent of the Main Thesis could still make use of the identification of singletons with singular haecceities.

[44] (Caplan, Tillman, and Reeder 2010) are not proponents of the Main Thesis; instead, they subscribe to Hierarchical Composition as we characterized it at the outset.

[45] This is a direct consequence of Proposition 3.2 according to which there is no total injective operation whereby one may assign a code to every object. The purpose of those codes, you may remember, had been to enable us to recover the codes uniquely from their fusions. Lewis' plan is to use singletons to play the role of codes.

[46] Armstrong (1995), in fact, hints at a restriction on the making of singletons in response to the limitative result reported by Rosen (1995).

logics. Indeed, the problem evaporates when one follows Florio and Linnebo (2021) and abandons one's adherence to instances of plural comprehension. While that might in the end be a live option, the purpose of next two sections is to check how far each horn of the dilemma might take one against the background of the current framework.

Let us look at each option in turn.

Classical Extensional Mereology Unbound

This is the strategy David Lewis pursues in *Parts of Classes*. One reason for the choice is that he regards the axioms of CEM as well understood, unproblematic, and certain. The part-to-whole relation is a topic-neutral relation that applies to all objects, regardless of their ontological category, and the operation of mereological composition is unmysterious and unrestricted.[47]

Since, for Lewis, the axioms of CEM are akin to the principles of logic, they should be accorded a similar level of generality. Given that these axioms are, for him, far better understood than the making of singletons has ever been, the choice is perfectly clear. It would, for Lewis, be unduly drastic to weaken mereology in order to keep the making of singletons, which is much less well understood, unbounded.

Lewis identifies MK as a mathematical target and makes a distinction between proper and improper classes or sets. What sets proper classes apart – in line with a distinction due to John von Neumann – is that they are not members, whence it follows that they do not have a singleton. So, Lewis' strategy fits well with a venerable account of the distinction between sets and classes, which he is able to recover in his system. But that means that the strategy inherits some of the difficulties generally associated with von Neumann's approach. In particular, we find that the nature of proper classes remains elusive. What exactly prevents a class from having a singleton and being a member? There is no completely satisfactory answer to this question. Instead, John von Neumann combined his distinction between sets and classes with a limitation of size hypothesis: a class is *proper* if, and only if, it is in one-to-one correspondence with the universal class. While this criterion helps us sort classes extensionally into proper and improper, it provides no explanation of the fact that such proper classes as the class of all classes or the class of all non–self-membered classes fail to be members of other classes. In other words, it is far from understood how exactly size alone would prevent the formation of a singleton for a proper class.

---

[47] He has an independent argument for this in Lewis (1986), which is known as the argument from vagueness.

The situation would have been different had we identified ZFC as a target. For that system posits no proper classes in addition to sets. But this is not on the cards for Lewis, who regards the axiom of fusion as unproblematic and certain. For an application of fusion will enable us to form the fusion of singletons of non–self-membered sets, which cannot itself be a set on pain of contradiction. Since the axiom of fusion is unnegotiable for Lewis, he has no choice but to countenance proper classes as well as sets.

Given the lack of special epistemic access to the nature of singletons, Lewis opts for a structuralist account of the nonmereological relation an object bears to its singleton, one which is designed to help us recover the axioms of MK. We no longer aspire to grasp the nature of *the* nonmereological relation an object bears to a singleton, but rather posit the existence of relations with the formal features required for a reconstruction of the theory of classes within mereology expanded with the theory of singletons.

One way to proceed is to introduce the concept of a *singleton function*, which is just a partial injection from objects to mereological atoms to which they bear the nonmereological relation in question. Lewis sets a number of formal constraints on singleton functions designed to help us recover the axioms of MK. These constraints are informed by the limitation of size hypothesis, which guarantees that the function is not defined on *large* fusions of singletons. To be more precise, a *singleton function* is, for Lewis, a partial injection s such that

- its range consists of mereological atoms called s-singletons
- its domain consists of *small* fusions of s-singletons and objects called s-individuals without s-singletons as parts
- all objects are generated from the s-individuals by iterated application of s and mereological fusion.

A fusion is *small* if and only if its atomic parts are *few* by which we mean, as usual, that they are not in one-to-one correspondence with all the atoms. Otherwise, the fusion is *large*. Notice that the distinctions of size should be understood in terms of the existence or nonexistence of certain functions, which means that they would involve quantification over functional relations in primitive notation.

The structuralist proposal is now to construe class-theoretic truths as covert generalizations over *singleton functions*; for example, to assert that membership is well-founded is to assert that whatever singleton function σ may be, the membership relation $\in_\sigma$ defined in terms of it is well-founded.[48] One problem at this point is that the expressive resources required to implement Lewis' strategy

---

[48] There is nothing special about well-founded set theory. Had we started with a consistent non–well-founded theory of sets and classes, we would have simply rewritten the axioms for the singleton operation differently.

appear to outstrip the plural formulation of classical mereology. As characterized earlier, class-theoretic truths require quantification over functions.
Quantification over functions boils down to quantification over functional
relations, but one may be tempted to simulate the latter in terms of plural
quantification over *ordered pairs*. The problem is that it is not clear how to
interpret talk of proper parts in the official framework of plural classical
mereology.

In collaboration with John Burgess and Allen Hazen, David Lewis explained
how to simulate quantification over binary relations in the framework of plural
quantification and mereology in the appendix to Lewis (1991). One method
requires the existence of an infinitude of atoms, even if reality does not consist
entirely of atoms. If, for simplicity, we assume that it does, we exploit
a consequence of the axiom of choice whereby an infinite domain of atoms A
may be decomposed into three pairwise disjoint subdomains A_1, A_2, A_3 where
each of them is in one-to-one correspondence with the union of the other two.[49]
The one-to-one maps conceived in terms of plural quantification over two-atom
fusions (or *diatoms*) make sure that each atom a in A_3 has an image a_1 in A_1 and
one image a_2 in A_2. Given two atoms a and b in A_3, we code $\langle a, b \rangle$ as the two-
atom fusion of the images of a and b in A_1 and A_2, respectively: $a_1 + b_2$. Plural
quantification over such codes achieves the effect of quantification over relations of atoms. In order to generalize the procedure to cover relations of
nonatomic fusions of atoms, we just note that each fusion of atoms finds an
image in the fusion of A_1-images of its atoms and another one in the fusion of
A_2-images of its atoms. The order pair of two nonatomic fusions is therefore
coded by the relevant fusion of two images.

The appendix to Lewis (1991) discusses at least one more method to achieve
the effect of quantification over ordered pairs, and yet a third, hybrid method is
used in Lewis (1993). Burgess (2015) has recently observed that all such
methods make crucial use of the axiom of choice and suggested the use of
Hilbert's ϵ operator as yet a simpler procedure.

Once such a method is in place, Lewis is in a position to recover the axioms of
MK from basic hypotheses to do with the size of reality such as, for example,
that there are no more small fusions of mereological atoms than there are atoms.

So, Lewis explains how to retain the Main Thesis if we opt for a structuralist
account of singletons and trade a philosophically inscrutable singleton operation
for any operation satisfying formal constraints commonly associated with the
singleton operation. One concern at this point is that the appeal to structuralism
seems to undermine the motivation for the Main Thesis. For once we're prepared

---

[49] This is the method of double images in Lewis (1991), which Lewis attributes to John Burgess.

to embrace structuralism in order to overcome the mystery of the nonmerelogical link between objects and their singletons, we may as well use it to overcome the mystery of membership. Much as the proponent of the Main Thesis construes singletons as mereological atoms with further nonmereological structure, we could construe classes more generally as mereological atoms with nonmereological structure, which links the members with the class of which they are members. In other words, we trade the existence of a philosophically inscrutable relation of membership with the existence of binary relations that satisfy the formal constraints encoded by the axioms of set theory. But once we do this, we have no further use for the Main Thesis. There is no pressure to take classes to have the rich mereological structure the Main Thesis attributes to them; they may as well be mereological atoms for all we are concerned.

The Making of Singletons Unbound

In contrast to the structuralist approach to singletons, a reductive account may identify them with mereological atoms for which we have an independent characterization. The reductive account proceeds to explain the nonmereological link between an object and its singleton in terms of some better understood link between the object and the object with its singleton has been identified. For examples of such approaches, consider the identification of singletons with certain states of affairs, or universals, or haecceities, or tropes. Each identification results in a different account of the nonmereological link between an object and its singleton.

Perhaps the best known example of the reductive approach is the proposal Armstrong (1991) discusses. David Armstrong countenances states of affairs, which involve the exemplification of properties and relations by individuals. These states of affairs are mereological atoms, but they are nonmereologically complex: particulars and properties are *constituents* of states of affairs, which are nonetheless mereologically simple. He proceeds to identify singletons with certain states of affairs of which the members of the singletons are constituents. In particular, Armstrong takes the object to be a *constituent* of the state of affairs, which consists of the object exemplifying unithood. This, in turn, is a second-order property an object exemplifies just in case it satisfies some unit-making property under which exactly *one* object of a certain sort is supposed to fall. Armstrong offers *weighting exactly one kilogram* as an example of a unit-making property since when presented with an instance, we judge that there is exactly one object of that sort.

The identification of singletons with states of affairs makes singletons less inscrutable than Lewis takes them to be, but on the other hand, it results in a more liberal approach to the making of singletons. For each object a, whether an individual or a class, is an instance of *being a*, which is unit-determining. So, no matter what object a, there should be a state of affairs, which consists of the object's exemplification of unithood. Since states of affairs are mereologically simple, by Armstrong's lights, this suggests that the singleton operation provides a total injection of all objects into mereological atoms, which, as Rosen (1995) observed, clashes with one of our limitative results of the previous section.

In response to the limitative result, Armstrong (1995) suggests we revisit the presupposition that unit-determining properties are generally available. Quite independently of the limitative result, Armstrong observes that the world itself conceived as the totality of all being appears to form a unit, yet the suggestion that it has a singleton would entail that the world itself is a mere constituent of a wider state of affairs. One compromise is to retreat to the weaker claim that it is merely *possible* for the totality of all being to form a unit. Thus, for totality of all being to form a singleton is *not* for there to be a state of affairs, which consists of the totality of all being exemplifying unithood. There is no such thing. Instead, it is enough to acknowledge that the totality of all being *could have been* a constituent of a state of affairs which would constitute its singleton.

One may alternatively revisit CEM. This is the option Forrest (2002a) embraces when confronted with a version of the difficulty for his own reduction of singletons. He proposes to identify the singleton of an object x not with a state of affairs but rather with a certain trope the universe exemplifies, namely, *having x as a part*. Tropes are properties that are particular to some object; other objects may possess perfectly similar properties, but they are not identical to it. For the Main Thesis to remain viable, we must construe tropes as mereological atoms.

One important difference between this suggestion and the proposal Armstrong discusses is that the trope in question is not required to have the universe as a constituent; instead, the trope itself is part of the universe. The nonmereological relation an object bears to a singleton and suggests the object is ultimately tracked by a trope exemplified by the universe. The proposal is close to one David Lewis explicitly considers in Lewis (1991, p. 56, n. 13) on which singletons are identified with self-identity tropes in the manner of D. C. Williams.

Whatever tropes we choose to play the role of singletons, we now have a total map from objects into mereological atoms, which, given Proposition 3.2, is inconsistent with CEM.[50] Forrest (2002a) suggests we appeal to the priority of

---

[50] On minimal assumptions such as the existence of at least two objects.

objects to the tropes they exemplify in order to motivate a restriction of the axiom of fusion. One rationale for this is that the identity conditions for tropes are specified in terms of the very objects that instantiate them. No sense is to be made of the trope without a prior specification of their instances. That appears to justify, for example, the absence of a fusion C of all classes, since such a fusion C would include every singleton as a part, including its own singleton $\{C\}$. But if $\{C\}$ is part of C, then it would have to be prior to the trope *being identical with* C, which would make $\{C\}$ prior to itself. Better to restrict the axiom of fusion in order to accommodate the fact that an object is *prior* to its singleton.

One may suggest that mereological composition occurs in stages of a certain cumulative hierarchy. There is first a level of individuals without immediate parts and their singletons. At the next level, we find fusions of individuals and/ or singletons found at the earlier level, and so on. For a more compact formulation of the thesis, fusions of singletons are formed in levels. Given some individuals without parts and/or fusions found at some level, there is a fusion of them.[51] Part of the motivation for the strategy at hand is the hypothesis that the sole member of a given singleton is *prior* to the singleton, but there are alternative moves available even for theorists for whom singletons and their members are on a par.

Different characterizations of CEM suggest different strategies to avoid paradox. Cotnoir and Varzi (2021) present CEM as Core Mereology + Remainder + Join, and one may be tempted to weaken remainder to strong supplementation in order to defuse the limitative constraint set in Proposition 3.2. The suggestion, to be more precise, is to retreat from Classical Extensional Mereology to Extensional Mereology (EM) + Join.[52] Figure 1 illustrates the fact that the system that results is strictly weaker than CEM, since it depicts a model of EM + Join that is not a model of CEM.

Each arrow in Figure 1 represents the relation a proper part bears to an object, but the diagram leaves implicit the fact that every object is a part of itself.

Remainder fails in the model because nothing in the model is a fusion of parts of d that fail to overlap a. This is precisely the feature one may hope to use in order to avoid paradox. For there is no reason to expect a join of atoms to have a unique decomposition into atoms; d, for example, is both the join of atoms a and b and that of b and c.

Consider now the case of the non–self-membered classes. There are non–self-membered classes, and they each come with a singleton. The singletons of

---

[51] This is in line with the proposal Caplan, Tillman, and Reeder (2010) outline, except for the fact that they are concerned with a different mereological operation.

[52] Recall that Extensional Mereology (EM) is Core Mereology + Strong Supplementation.

Figure 1 A model of EM + Join

the non–self-membered classes have a join, R, but R is not a fusion of them, on pain of contradiction. For R has a singleton, $\{R\}$, which is part of R on pain of contradiction. (Otherwise, $R \notin R$, and $\{R\}$ would have to be a part of R.) But $\{R\}$ is not an atom of a non–self-membered class; the join of singletons of non–self-membered classes, R, includes a part distinct from them. So, R is a class of all, but not only, non–self-membered classes: R contains at least one self-membered class, namely, R itself, on pain of contradiction.[53]

There are very simple models of the framework in which the making of singletons remains unbounded.[54] The question, of course, is whether it is more generally able to support a rich and varied domain of classes. The answer is mixed. On the one hand, nothing prevents the construction of more elaborate models in which a vast array of individuals are asked to play the role of proper classes. On the other hand, there are serious limits as to how much comprehension the models can accommodate. In particular, the axiom of join is inconsistent with simple instances of predicative class comprehension formulated in

---

[53] Or consider Mirimanoff's paradox, which arises when we consider the join of the well-founded classes. There are well-founded classes, and they each come with a singleton. The singletons of well-founded classes have a join, W, which is not their fusion on pain of contradiction. For otherwise, W itself would be well-founded, in which case its singleton, $\{W\}$, would have to be one of its parts. That would make W self-membered and non–well-founded. So, W is not a fusion of singletons of well-founded classes, which means that it overlaps some singleton of some non–well-founded class.

[54] Given an individual Ω, we may start with a model of ZFCU of the form

$$\langle V_\kappa(\{\Omega\}), \in, S \rangle,$$

where κ is a strong inaccessible κ and $S = V_\kappa(\{\Omega\})\backslash\{\Omega\}$. We will define a relation of part on $V_\kappa(\{\Omega\})$. First, we identify the set of atomic classes of the model, $A = \{\{x\} : x \in V_\kappa(\{\Omega\})\}$, and the joins of sets of atomic classes in the model, $J = V_\kappa(\{\Omega\})\backslash\{\varnothing\}$. We now define the operation $\gamma : \mathrm{P}^{<\kappa}(A)\backslash\{\varnothing\} \rightarrow J$:

$$\gamma(X) = \begin{cases} \bigcup X & \text{if } |X| < \kappa \\ \Omega & \text{if } |X| = \kappa \end{cases}.$$

We now define a relation that specifies the atomic classes that are parts of a given member of the domain, $x \leq^- y := \exists Y \subseteq A(y = \gamma(Y) \wedge x \in Y)$. This enables us to define a relation of part to whole in the model: $x \leq y : (y \in J \wedge \forall z(z \leq^- x \rightarrow z \leq^- y)) \vee (y = \varnothing \wedge x = y)$. We now define membership in the model: $x \,\epsilon\, y := \{x\} \leq y$, and $Sx := \exists y\, y \,\epsilon\, x \vee x = \varnothing$. Notice that ϵ extends the member relation in the model $\in$. One reason the model is trivial is that there is a single proper class in the model, Ω, which is the join of both the set of non–self-membered classes, all classes, all von Neumann ordinals, etc.

a typed two-sorted language in which we bar atomic formulas of the form $X \in y$ and $X \in Y$:

$$\exists X \forall x (x \in X \leftrightarrow \varphi(x)),$$

where $\varphi(x)$ contains no bound class variables. Given Join, we abandon instances of predicative comprehension of the form:

$$\exists X \forall x (x \in X \leftrightarrow x \neq y),$$

where y is a free set variable.[55] That means that some *sets* must fail to form a class in the presence of Join.

Proper Classes

What animates Lewis (1991) and Lewis (1993) is the ambition to explain what is for something to be a member in terms of singleton and part. There is, however, a very different motivation one may provide in support of the Main Thesis. Set theory presupposes a distinction between sets and classes, but there are at least two different attitudes one may take with respect to that distinction. We've thus far remained neutral with respect to whether nonempty sets are special cases of classes or whether the distinction corresponds to two fundamentally different types of collection. This is the distinction Burgess (2004) draws between *lumpers* and *splitters*. Lewis (1991) and Lewis (1993) take the view of a *lumper* for whom there is a broad category of collection under which classes fall, and nonempty sets are just some of them. Sets are, for the lumper, classes that are, in fact, members, whereas proper classes are never members.

Splitters, on the other hand, deny that every nonempty set is, in fact, a class. For each nonempty set, there is a coextensive class, one whose members are exactly the elements of the set. But there is no reason to take coextensiveness to be sufficient for identity. If, as suggested in Uzquiano (2003) and Boolos (1984), to speak of a class is just to speak of the members in the plural, then the plurality of elements of the set is coextensive with the set. But to the extent to which the set is one while the class may be many, it is not open to one to identify them. Set theory is concerned with the element–set relation, which is governed by the axioms of ZFC. Classes, on the other hand, are fundamentally

---

[55] Consider the condition:

$$\exists y (x = \{\{y\}\} \wedge \{\{y\}\} \not\leq y).$$

Let $R = \vee \exists y (x = \{\{y\}\} \wedge \{\{y\}\} \not\leq y)$. On the one hand, $\{\{R\}\} \leq R$. (This is because $\{\{R\}\} \not\leq R$ only if $\{\{R\}\} \leq R$.) On the other hand, suppose $\forall x (x \in X \leftrightarrow x \neq \{R\})$. If $\{\{x\}\} \not\leq x$, then $x \neq R$, $\{x\} \neq \{R\}$. So, $\{x\} \in X$ and $\{\{x\}\} \leq X$. Since R is a join of all such sets, $R \leq X$ and thus $\{\{R\}\} \leq R \leq X$, which means $\{\{R\}\} \leq X$ and $\{R\} \in X$, which means $\{R\} \neq \{R\}$. Contradiction. Thanks to Sam Roberts here.

different from sets, and the theory of classes studies the interaction between the element–set relation and the relation a member bears to a class. Unlike sets, classes are never members and they satisfy comprehension principles that posit the existence of a class of all and only sets satisfying a certain condition.[56] Others may insist on an interpretation of classes on which they are objects with members but they are never sets.[57] The issue for such theorists is to explain the mysterious distinction they draw between what look like two fundamentally different sorts of collection: sets and classes.

When pressed to explain the distinction between sets and classes, one may initially be tempted to take a step back and make do without proper classes. That would allow one to vindicate the thought that as Boolos (1984) puts it, ZFC is the most comprehensive theory of collections. The problem is that proper classes have earned their keep in set theory. On the one hand, they provide the means to reformulate the axiom schemas of separation and replacement as single axioms, which enables one to produce a finite axiomatization of set theory. On the other hand, they have played a role in the motivation of large cardinal axioms.[58]

There is prima facie reason to take talk of proper classes at face value, and the problem of proper classes becomes the challenge to provide an account of the distinction between sets and classes on which following Maddy (1983), proper classes are sufficiently different from sets, but they nevertheless remain as real and well-defined as sets. Extant accounts of proper classes often deliver on one constraint at the expense of the other. Maddy (1983) explains how the likes of von Neumann, Morse, Kelley, and Reinhardt strive to make classes real, well-defined entities, but their classes look suspiciously similar to sets. Others understand talk of classes in terms of satisfaction of open formulas of the language of set theory relative to appropriate set parameters or even in terms of plural quantification over sets. These accounts make classes significantly different from sets, but they dispense with classes conceived as objects in the range of our first-order variables.

This is fertile ground for a mereological interpretation of classes with the Main Thesis as a centerpiece. One option that emerges is to identify classes with mereological sums of sets against the background of the Main Thesis. There is a distinction to be made between, for example, the unordered pair $\{a, b\}$ and the

---

[56] NBG restricts attention to conditions whose variables range exclusively over sets, whereas MK allows for impredicative conditions that quantify over classes in addition to sets.
[57] Horsten and Welch (2016) want classes to be objects in order to make sense of reflection principles whereby the set-theoretic universe is compared with certain proper initial segments thereof.
[58] See, for example, Uzquiano (2003) and Horsten and Welch (2016).

mereological sum $\{a\} + \{b\}$, which, on the view at hand, is *not* a set, but rather a class. Its parts, however, are its subclasses, namely, $\{a\}$ and $\{b\}$. Singleton sets provide the atomic constituents for classes, which have them as parts. Singleton classes are in fact sets, but not all *improper* classes are: complex mereological sums of singletons have sets as proper atomic parts but they may have further proper parts as well.

This is the general approach to the problem of proper classes Horsten and Welch (2016) and Horsten (2016) have recently articulated. One important difference with respect to Lewis (1991) and Lewis (1993) is that they do not share Lewis' ambition to explain the element–set relation in terms of a more fundamental relation. Instead, they take sets as given and the element–set relation as antecedently understood, and they seek to understand the relation a member bears to a class in terms of the element–set relation: to be a member of a class is nothing other than to be an element of an atomic part of a class, namely, a singleton set.

The mereological interpretation of proper classes vindicates the thought that ZFC is the most comprehensive theory of collections, where collections are conceived as sets formed at stages of a cumulative hierarchy. The set-theoretic universe is *the* mereological sum of all singletons, and, unlike sets, it is not formed at a stage of the cumulative hierarchy. Other parts of the set-theoretic universe correspond to other proper classes. Classes, for them, are parts of the set-theoretic universe, and for a class to be part of another is just for the former to be a subclass of the latter. Against the background of CEM, their account vindicates an impredicative form of class comprehension, which delivers a rich and varied domain of classes that supports their applications in set theory.

The account of proper classes as mereological sums of singletons appears to deliver on two constraints Maddy (1983) identified for a satisfactory solution to the problem of proper classes. On the one hand, mereological sums are real well-defined objects; indeed, they lie in the range of our first-order variables and they fall within the subject matter of mereology. And, on the other, mereological sums are significantly different from sets. To the extent to which the operation of mereological composition seems structurally different from that of set formation, there may be some reason to expect their outputs to be different.[59] Horsten and Welch (2016) and Horsten (2016) take for granted that proper classes are never elements; there is, for example, no opportunity to form a singleton of the class of all sets. On their view, unlike sets, classes are not *mathematical objects*, and as parts of the mathematical universe, they

---

[59] To illustrate the structural differences between the two operations, notice that the mereological sum of some sums of parts, for example, is nothing over and above the sum of the given parts. Yet, the set of sets of some members is a new set, one which contains each of the sets in question.

themselves are never available for set formation at any stage of the cumulative hierarchy.

There is, however, room for an alternative conception of proper classes. If proper classes are indeed well-defined objects, which are *not* sets, they appear to qualify as *urelements*. The elements of their singleton parts are *members* of each class, but being a member of a class is different from being an element of a set. Now, to the extent to which proper classes may be conceived as *urelements*, they should be available for set formation at the very first stage of the cumulative hierarchy: we should be able to form a singleton of the class of all classes as well as further sets of classes.

One consequence of this view is that there is no longer reason to think that there should be a set of *urelements*.[60] There is, however, no decisive obstacle for the development of impure set theory with a proper class of urelements. Indeed, Zermelo himself appears to make allowance for a failure of the urelements to form a set in Zermelo (1930). Nor is it clear that the iterative conception of set requires a set of urelements at the very first state of the cumulative hierarchy.[61]

More serious is the clash with the limitative constraint discussed in connection to Proposition 3.2. Once we make allowance for proper classes to play the role of urelements available for collection into further sets, we turn the singleton operation into a total injective map from the domain of all objects into the range of mereological atoms. That, we know, is inconsistent with CEM, which means that we are under pressure to weaken the mereological framework again. Our discussion of the main responses available to reductionist accounts of the singleton operation carry over to this case.

5 Hierarchical Composition

We now shift focus on the hypothesis that classes exhibit a hierarchical mereological structure: they are composed of their members, some of which may themselves be composed of further members. One version of the hypothesis identifies the proper parts of a given class with its members, the members of its members, etc. If there are individuals in the transitive closure of a class, then their proper parts are similarly proper parts of the class. Unless a subclass is itself a member of the given class, then it is not counted as a part of the class. There is, however, a more liberal formulation of the hypothesis that includes the

---

[60] Barwise and Moss (1996), McGee (1997), and Menzel (2014) discuss the axiom that there is a set of *urelements* along with some applications.

[61] See Uzquiano (2015b) for some discussion of this point.

subclasses of the given class as some of its parts. Classes are composed of members, but they are likewise composed of their subclasses.

We look at two implementations of the proposal set against different mereological frameworks. One of them, which is due to Forrest (2002b), construes the relation of part as basic and attempts to mimic member in terms of the relation of maximal proper part against the background of Heyting mereology. This approach to immediate part enables one to define a surrogate for the member relation, which Forrest (2002b) calls a *pseudomember* relation. Despite some limitations, there is one important respect in which the theory of *pseudoclasses* provides a framework within which to recover much of set theory – provided at least that the domain of individuals is sufficiently rich and varied. While Forrest (2002b) takes the more liberal perspective on Hierarchical Composition, it is not difficult to modify the account in order to accommodate the strict formulation of Hierarchical Composition.

The other option is to ignore the qualm that immediate part is not a transitive relation and nonetheless adopt that relation as a basic mereological primitive. The mereological background for this proposal is an axiomatization of hierarchical mereology in terms of immediate part. Caplan, Tillman, and Reeder (2010) proceed to identify a class with a *rigid embodiment* of its members as they exemplify some attribute or another.[62] Singletons are special cases of classes; for them, the singleton $\{a\}$ is a rigid embodiment of the object a as it exemplifies some attribute or another.[63] While the proposal is consistent with the strict formulation of Hierarchical Composition, it is not difficult to adapt the account in order to accommodate more liberal formulations of the hypothesis on which subclasses are indeed counted as parts of a given class.

A Theory of Pseudoclasses

We introduced Heyting mereology as a candidate axiomatization of part for a proponent of the hierarchical perspective on composition.

One of the distinctive features of Heyting mereology is that an object may be more than the join of its proper parts, for example, $\{a\}$ is, on the face of it, *more than a*, which is the join of the proper parts of $\{a\}$. Once we relinquish weak supplementation, we must draw a distinction between simplicity understood as

---

[62] Caplan, Tillman, and Reeder (2010) coin the term 'Fine part' to refer to what we have called immediate part, and they explicitly address the question of whether its nontransitivity is a reason to think it is not a relation of part to whole.

[63] In this case, the material part of the singleton would be a, and its formal part would be the principle of embodiment. If, following Caplan, Tillman, and Reeder (2010), you identify the empty set with the latter, you will have a view on which singletons are rigid embodiments composed of their sole member and the empty set conceived as an attribute, one which provides the principle of embodiment whereby the singleton is generated from a given object.

the lack of proper parts and atomicity construed as the lack of a decomposition into proper parts. For there are now at least two different reasons for an object to lack such a decomposition. A *simple* is, of course, not a join or proper parts, but neither is an object with a single maximal proper part, for example, $\{a\}$. To the extent to which $\{a\}$ lacks a decomposition into proper parts, we may conceive of it as a mereological *atom* even if it is not a simple. If there are classes, then singletons are nonsimple atoms. The singleton of a, $\{a\}$, is no longer simple because it has a as a proper part, indeed, a maximal proper part.

The other important feature of the framework is that part is construed as basic and other mereological relations are to explained in terms of part. The crucial question now is how to characterize the relation of immediate part in terms of part. One proposal we mentioned at the outset is to make do with the relation of maximal proper part:

$$x \lhd y := x < y \wedge \neg \exists z (x < z \wedge z < y).$$

(Simons 1987)(108) and Cotnoir and Varzi (2021, sec. 3.3.2) discuss the proposal in detail.[64] Given Hierarchical Composition, each of two members a and b would be maximal proper parts of the class $\{a, b\}$: they each would be proper parts of $\{a, b\}$, and none of them would be proper parts of further proper parts of $\{a, b\}$. But whatever its merits, that would still not be the relation of immediate part at play in the hypothesis that classes exhibit a hierarchical mereological structure. For as Fine (1992) observes, we would like to count a as an immediate part of $\{a, \{a\}\}$ even after we acknowledge that it is *not* a maximal proper part of that class. Given Hierarchical Composition, a is a proper part of $\{a\}$, which is, in turn, a proper part of $\{a, \{a\}\}$. Therefore, a is not a maximal proper part of $\{a, \{a\}\}$.

Matters are similar for Liberal Hierarchical Composition on which sub-classes are counted as parts of a given class. Once we let subclasses such as $\{a\}$ and $\{b\}$ be parts of the class $\{a, b\}$, we are forced to acknowledge that a is not even a maximal proper part of $\{a, b\}$. For on the liberal formulation of the hypothesis, a is a proper part of $\{a\}$, which is itself counted as a proper part of $\{a, b\}$. So, maximal proper part is not quite what we want if we want to mimic the relation a member bears to a class. One temporary fix may be to focus on a similar relation:

$$x \unlhd y := \exists z (x \lhd z \wedge z \leq y).$$

Here $z \leq y$ abbreviates $z < y \vee z = y$. Neither a nor b would be maximal proper parts of the class $\{a, b\}$, but they each qualify as a maximal proper part of *some*

---

[64] Goodman (2022) entertains a similar proposal except for the further stipulation that y is not matter.

part of $\{a,b\}$, namely, $\{a\}$ and $\{b\}$, respectively. But we face a similar diffi-culty. For notice that we now have that $a \trianglelefteq \{\{a\}\}$, since a is a maximal proper part of some part of $\{\{a\}\}$, namely, $\{a\}$. Unfortunately, we do not want to count a as an immediate part of $\{\{a\}\}$ even after we acknowledge that it is a maximal proper part of some part of that class.

One approach at this point is to persevere and seek to find a more appropri-ate surrogate for the member relation defined in terms of part. This is the strategy Forrest (2002b) pursues when he defines a *pseudomember* relation in terms of $\trianglelefteq$:

$$xEy := x \trianglelefteq y \wedge \neg \exists z (x \trianglelefteq z \wedge z \trianglelefteq y).$$

That is, x is a *pseudomember* of y if x is a maximal part of some part of y, but x is *not* a maximal part of any part of y that is itself a maximal part of some part of y. While, much like before, $a \trianglelefteq \{\{a\}\}$, we are now in a position to rule a out as a pseudomember of $\{\{a\}\}$ since $a \trianglelefteq \{a\}$ and $\{a\} \trianglelefteq \{\{a\}\}$.

In line with Forrest (2002b), define a *pseudoset* as something with pseudo-members, which is itself a pseudomember of something; and a *pseudoclass* is something with pseudomembers, which is itself *not* a pseudomember. This is of course perfectly parallel to von Neumann's distinction between sets and classes, except for the fact that we now have reasons of principle to expect some pseudoclasses to never be pseudomembers. For suppose that U contains all pseudosets as pseudomembers; then U should be a pseudoclass: for otherwise, if U has a pseudosingleton u, then $U E u$ and $U \trianglelefteq u$.[65] On the other hand, if v is a pseudosingleton of u, then $u \trianglelefteq v$ and $v \trianglelefteq U$, which would contradict the fact that uEU since, by hypothesis, U contains all peudosets as pseudomembers.

The project now is to lay down a theory of pseudoclasses and to investigate the extent to which they provide surrogates for classes and serve as a foundation for vast parts of mathematics. It turns out that provided a rich supply of individuals, the theory of pseudoclasses will have the means to interpret pure set theory, and will therefore serve a variety of foundational purposes.

There are at least two prima facie obstacles facing the formulation of a theory of pseudoclasses, but none of them turn out to be decisive. One problem is that unlike $\in$, the newly introduced pseudomember relation ϵ is *not* extensional. If there are classes, then it is not difficult to verify that $\{\{a\}\}$ and $\{a, \{a\}\}$ share exactly the same pseudomembers, that is, $\{a\}$. For $a \trianglelefteq \{a\}$ and we have each $\{a\} \trianglelefteq \{\{a\}\}$ and $\{a\} \trianglelefteq \{a, \{a\}\}$.[66] The nonextensional character of the pseu-domember relation makes it difficult to speak of *the* pseudosingleton of a given

---

[65] To be a singleton of U is to have U as the sole pseudomember.

[66] The latter is just because $\{a\} \triangleleft \{\{a\}\}$ and $\{\{a\}\} \leq \{a, \{a\}\}$.

individual a, as there may be more than one pseudoset with a as its sole pseudomember.

We may rephrase the problem differently. Let us introduce *pseudoclass abstracts* of the form

$$[x : \varphi(x)]$$

in the hope that they might refer to pseudoclasses x, whose pseudomembers are exactly the objects that satisfy the relevant condition $\varphi(x)$. That is,

$$\forall y(yE[x : \varphi(x)] \leftrightarrow \varphi(y)).$$

Let us stipulate, as usual, that $[a]$ is a pseudoclass whose only pseudomember is a, $[a, [b]]$ is a pseudoclass whose pseudomembers are exactly a and the pseudoclass $[b]$, and so on. One issue is that the fact that ϵ is not extensional undermines the presumption that there is at most one candidate referent for each pseudoclass abstract $[a]$. This is not an insurmountable obstacle according to Forrest (2002b). One option is to regard the reference of pseudoclass abstracts as referentially indeterminate: there is an oversupply of referents, which may be accommodated through the use of supervaluations. Even if pseudoclass abstracts are referentially indeterminate, the class-theoretic statements in which they appear may nevertheless receive a determinate truth value, since they are not sensitive to class-theoretic irrelevant differences between the candidate referents for each pseudoclass abstract.

There is another alternative, which is simply to make an arbitrary choice in each case. Hilbert's ϵ-symbol seems tailor-made for this purpose. As Burgess (2015) notes, one common pattern in mathematics after one satisfies oneself of the existence of at least one witness to a given condition $\varphi(x)$ is to introduce a term τ to refer to such an object. The Hilbert ϵ-symbol codifies this procedure formally through the introduction of a singular term $\epsilon x \varphi(x)$ under certain conditions to denote one instance of the condition.[67] We could take the symbol to be governed by the principles:

$$\exists x \varphi(x) \rightarrow \varphi(\epsilon x . \varphi(x))$$
$$\forall x(\varphi(x) \leftrightarrow \psi(x)) \rightarrow \epsilon x . \varphi(x) = \epsilon x . \psi(x).$$

So, if something satisfies the formula $\forall y(yEx \leftrightarrow \varphi(y))$, we could let $\epsilon x \forall y(yEx \leftrightarrow \varphi(y))$ denote one such object. We may in such cases construe the pseudoclass abstract as a suitable Hilbert term:

$$[x : \varphi(x)] := \epsilon x \forall y(yEx \leftrightarrow \varphi(y)).$$

---

[67] Burgess (2015) makes the proposal in the context of Lewis' proposed reduction of the theory of classes to classical mereology and the theory of singletons.

If the nonextensional character of E is a threat to uniqueness, there is an even more serious threat to existence. For there is no a priori guarantee for the existence of a witness to the generalization:

$$\forall y(yEx \leftrightarrow \varphi(y)).$$

Indeed, as Forrest (2002b) points out, the existence of such a witness is sometimes *refutable*. Given an individual a and a pseudoclass $[a, b]$, there is nothing to satisfy the formula:

$$\forall y(yEx \leftrightarrow y = a \lor y = [a, b]).$$

For such a pseudoclass $[a, [a, b]]$, if it existed, would contain a and $[a, b]$ as pseudomembers: $aE[a, [a, b]]$ and $[a, b]E[a, [a, b]]$. That would mean that $a \trianglelefteq [a, [a, b]]$ and $[a, b] \trianglelefteq [a, [a, b]]$, which, by definition, rules a out as a pseudomember of the class: $\neg aE[a, [a, b]]$. We conclude that $[a, [a, b]]$ fails to denote a pseudoclass on pain of contradiction.

This raises the question of whether the domain of pseudoclasses is sufficiently rich and varied to be of mathematical interest and to sustain a measure of set theory and mathematics. Remarkably, Forrest (2002b) observes that the framework has the resources to provide pseudosets for a rich variety of well-founded sets, which he calls *simply well-founded sets*. Given a set $\{a, \{b, c\}\}$, we may use a directed graph to represent the relation of member on the transitive closure of $\{a, \{b, c\}\}$. Each edge represents the converse of the member relation: an arrow from a node m to a node n represents the fact that the set n represents a member of the set m represents. We will in that case refer to n as a *child* of m. The top node of the graph corresponds to the set we want to represent, and the other nodes in the graph correspond to sets in the transitive closure of the initial set. A *path* is a sequence of nodes where each node is a child of its predecessor. The graph in question will be a *tree* if no two nodes are connected by more than one path. For a visual representation, compare the graph for the set $\{a, \{b, c\}\}$, namely, Figure 2, which is indeed a tree, with the graph for the set $\{a, \{a, b\}\}$, namely, Figure 3, which is not:

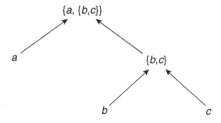

Figure 2 A graph for $\{a, \{b, c\}\}$.

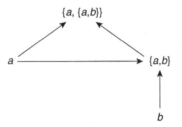

Figure 3 A graph for $\{a, \{a, b\}\}$.

The arrows in each of the preceding graphs represent the membership relation on the transitive closure of each set. The graph for $\{a, \{b, c\}\}$ is a tree because no two nodes are connected by more than one path. On the other hand, the graph for $\{a, \{a, b\}\}$ is *not* a tree because there is more than one path from a to $\{a, \{a, b\}\}$: one connects a directly to $\{a, \{a, b\}\}$, whereas the other proceeds indirectly via $\{a, b\}$. Nor is there a tree corresponding to the restriction of the member relation to the transitive closure of $\{\{b, c\}, \{c, d\}\}$ as represented in Figure 4.

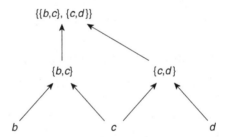

Figure 4 A graph for $\{\{b, c\}, \{c, d\}\}$.

The reason this time is that there is more than one path connecting c to $\{\{b, c\}, \{c, d\}\}$: one via $\{b, c\}$ and the other via $\{c, d\}$.

Forrest's simply well-founded sets are those for which the graph corresponding to the restriction of the member relation to their transitive closure forms a tree. One crucial observation at this point is that the framework provides a pseudoset for each simply well-founded set, whose parts form a model of Heyting mereology.

To be sure, pure sets are generally *not* simply well-founded, for example, $\{\varnothing, \{\varnothing\}\}$ whose graph is given in Figure 5. But given a sufficiently rich and varied domain of individuals, we may make do with simply well-founded impure sets. For we may, if we like, map each *pure set* into a simply well-founded *impure set* when we let different individuals play the role of $\varnothing$ in different nodes of the graph for the pure set. So, given two individuals a and b, the role of $\{\varnothing, \{\varnothing\}\}$ could be played by the simply well-founded impure set $\{a, \{b\}\}$, whose graph is given in Figure 6.

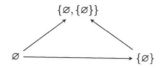

Figure 5 A graph for $\{\varnothing, \{\varnothing\}\}$

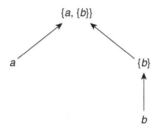

Figure 6 A graph for $\{a, \{b\}\}$

Since a von Neumann ordinal contains all of its predecessors as members, von Neumann ordinals are not simply well-founded. But given a countable number of individuals, we have a simply well-founded impure set to play the role of ω, where each occurrence of ω in the graph is replaced with a different individual. It is not difficult to check that we will require an inaccessible domain of individuals in order to be able to count on simply well-founded impure surrogates for all the ordinals less than the first inaccessible, whose existence is guaranteed by the axioms of ZFC.

Rigid Embodiments

One motivation for the theory of pseudoclasses is the ability to make do with a basic relation of part without further nonmereological primitives. The relation of pseudomember is defined in terms of part alone, and unlike the approach discussed in the previous section, there is no use for a primitive singleton function. But the price is high, since however fruitful, the relation of pseudo-member is at most an inadequate surrogate for the more basic relation of member. This is the point of the departure for the next proposal.

What we learn when we attempt to characterize the relation of immediate part in terms of maximal proper part is that the former is not adequately captured against the background of Heyting mereology where part is construed as the basic mereological relation. The fact that an individual a is not a maximal proper part of the class $\{a, \{a\}\}$ reveals that not all immediate parts are maximal proper parts, and the fact that $\{a, \{a\}\}$ and $\{\{a\}\}$ share the same maximal proper parts suggests that immediate part is not to be defined in terms of part alone.

One option at this juncture is to shift from the relation of part to that of immediate part as the basic mereological relation and to formulate an axiomatization of hierarchical mereology in terms of the latter. We explained how to do that in Section 3, and we are now in a position to develop the theory of classes against that background. The mereological framework is a variation of the system Fine (1999) formulated in terms of immediate part in line with Jacinto and Cotnoir (2019). Hierarchical mereology codifies the hierarchical conception of composition on which objects submit to a hierarchical decomposition into immediate parts, each of which may have further immediate parts. Each complex object consists of some immediate parts unified by a certain form, which some theorists call a "principle of unity," for example, Johnston (2006), and others identify with a relation or an attribute, for example, Fine (1999). Classes are a special instance of this phenomenon. They submit to a hierarchical decomposition into members, which are their immediate parts, some of which may have further members as immediate parts. What unifies the immediate parts of a class, however, is the existence of its members, which Johnston (2006) understands as a multigrade relation which applies to some objects if, and only if, they all exist. Caplan, Tillman, and Reeder (2010) propose to understand the unity of a class in terms of the satisfaction of some attribute or another. However one conceives of a class, the relation of member may now be characterized as a special instance of the relation of immediate part when restricted to the domain of classes.

We now operate in the plural formulation of hierarchical mereology formulated at the end of Section 3. Let E be the plural attribute some objects xx exemplify if, and only if, they all exist. Given a modal operator $\square$ for metaphysical necessity, at the very least, we assume

$$\square\left(Exx \leftrightarrow \forall x(x \prec xx \rightarrow \exists y\, x = y)\right).$$

Given some objects xx, the rigid embodiment they compose as they exist, xx/E, shares its immediate constituents with a variety of other rigid embodiments, for example, the rigid embodiment they compose as they exemplify a certain spatial arrangement, xx/S. But one key difference between them is that their existence conditions are linked to the existence conditions of the given objects regardless of what other attributes they may exemplify. In this respect, xx/E is a better candidate to play the role of $\{a, b\}$ than xx/S when S is a spatial attribute the objects may exemplify at one time/world but not at another.

We now define a class as a rigid embodiment of some objects xx/E as they exist, and we define the relation a member bears to a class in terms of immediate part. In other words:

$$CX \quad := \quad \exists xx \ X = xx/E$$
$$x \in Y \quad := \quad x \ll Y \wedge CY.$$

The relation of member inherits the irreflexivity, asymmetry, and antitransitivity of immediate part. On the other hand, one important difference between member and immediate part is that unlike the latter, the former is extensional:

$$\forall x(x \in X \leftrightarrow x \in Y) \to X = Y.$$

This follows from the definition of class in combination with plural identity postulate (PR3):

$$\exists x \ x = xx/X \to (xx/X = yy/Y \leftrightarrow xx \approx yy \wedge X = Y).$$

When we restrict attention to classes, we obtain:

$$\exists x \ x = xx/E \to (xx/E = yy/E \leftrightarrow xx \approx yy),$$

which means that two classes are identical if they share the same immediate parts, which means that they are coextensive.

While we are broadly on the path Caplan, Tillman, and Reeder (2010) laid when they set out to identify classes with certain rigid embodiments, there are some differences as well. One difference concerns the principle of unity of classes, which, for them, is a higher-order multigrade attribute *exemplifying some attribute or another*. This is, as they conceive of it, an attribute some objects exemplify just in case they exemplify some attribute or relation, and, much like E, it is one the objects in question will exemplify whenever they exist. The other important difference is that their preferred axiomatization of hierarchical mereology explicitly includes the attribute that unifies a rigid embodiment as one of its immediate parts, indeed much like Fine (1999), they make a distinction between the *material* immediate parts of a rigid embodiment and the *formal* immediate part that unifies them.[68] That means that they regard the attribute E as one of the immediate parts of a class, and they exploit this observation to provide their own original account of the empty set, $\emptyset$, which they identify with an attribute. The empty set is thus an immediate, albeit a formal, part of all classes, indeed part of all singletons.

The outlook that emerges is in line with Hierarchical Composition, since to be a proper part of a given class is to be an ancestral immediate part of the class.

---

[68] Their formulation of iterative composition in Caplan, Tillman, and Reeder (2010, p. 513) makes the commitment explicit.

That includes the members of the class, the members of its members, the members of the members of its members, and so on. And it includes the immediate parts of individuals that are parts of the class. That means that not all subclasses are counted as parts: $\{a\}$ is a subclass of $\{a, b\}$, but it is certainly not one of its immediate parts. One may be tempted to point out that each immediate material part of $\{a\}$ is an immediate material part of $\{a, b\}$, but absent some principle of supplementation, that observation would not, by itself, help us establish that one is part of the other. In that respect, the proposal agrees with Caplan, Tillman, and Reeder (2010), which is consistent with Hierachical Composition.

One question at this point is whether one may adopt some variation on the present proposal in order to vindicate Liberal Hierachical Composition, which regards the subclasses of a given class as some of its parts. We may find inspiration in (Fine 1999), who considers but does not officially adopt a criterion for part in terms of states of affairs:

$a, b, c, \ldots / R$ is part of $a', b', c', \ldots / R'$ if the state of $a, b, c, \ldots$ standing in the relation R is part of the state of $a', b', c' \ldots$ standing in the relation R'.[69]

This suggests a plural counterpart:

$xx/F = yy/G$ if part of what is for yy to be G is for xx to be F.

But what exactly is for some objects xx to be F to be part of what is for some objects yy to be G? At the very least, necessarily, if yy are G, then xx are F, which would in turn invite a modal formulation of the principle:

$$\Box\,(Gyy \rightarrow Fxx) \rightarrow xx/F \leq yy/G.$$

When restricted to classes, the principle collapses into:

$$\Box\,(Eyy \rightarrow Exx) \rightarrow xx/E \leq yy/E.$$

But this, in turn, suggests that subclasses are themselves parts of classes:

$$xx \preccurlyeq yy \rightarrow \Box\,(Eyy \rightarrow Exx)$$
$$\Box\,(Eyy \rightarrow Exx) \rightarrow xx/E \rightarrow yy/E.$$

That is, part of what is for a, b, c to exemplify E is for a, b to itself exemplify E. (Had a, b not existed, one of them would have not existed and a, b, c would have not existed either.) That would help secure the claim that $\{a, b\}$ is part of $\{a, b, c\}$, despite the fact that the former is neither an immediate part nor an ancestral immediate part of the latter. On the view that emerges, a class is

---

[69] See Fine (1999, p. 66).

a proper part of another if the former is either an ancestral immediate part or a subclass of the latter, which is in line with Liberal Hierarchical Composition.

One limitative constraint on hierarchical mereology is that we should restrict the existence postulate for rigid postulates on pain of contradiction.[70] One way to do this is make sure that rigid embodiments are composed in stages of a certain cumulative hierarchy. There is a first stage at which we find individuals without proper parts. At successor stages $\alpha + 1$, we form rigid embodiments composed of immediate parts found at stage α as they exemplify a plural attribute. At limit stages λ, we form rigid embodiments composed of immediate parts found at earlier stages $\beta < \lambda$ as they exemplify a plural attribute.[71] When we restrict attention to classes, we realize that they are no exception to the rule: classes are formed in stages. We begin with a domain of individuals without parts. At successor stages, we form classes of objects drawn from the earlier stage. Finally, at limit stages, we form classes of objects drawn from earlier stages in the hierarchy.

One apparent advantage of the proposal is that it provides independent motivation for the iterative conception of set as an instance of a broader phenomenon, one which is separate from the threat set-theoretic antinomies pose to the principle of naive comprehension for set theory. Some may remain skeptical on the grounds that we had to modify the plural formulation of the existence postulate for rigid embodiments under duress: Proposition 3.3 tells us that the original postulate came into conflict with the plural formulation of Cantor's theorem. Indeed, one might have sought to weaken the axioms of plural quantification instead. That is precisely what Florio and Linnebo (2021) do when they advocate for a restriction of Plural Comprehension in order to accommodate Plural Collapse, which is just the thesis that no matter what some objects may be, they form a set.

But Fine (2010) offers in effect a separate rationale for the outlook. He characterizes an object as *prior* to another if the former appears in the explanation of the identity conditions of the latter. That is, in order to explain what the latter is, one must mention the former. The thought now is that the immediate parts of a rigid embodiment are *prior* to the embodiment. In order to explain *what* the rigid embodiment *is*, there is no choice but to mention its immediate parts and the attribute which unifies them. This relation of priority is, in fact, what underlies the formation of rigid embodiments in stages of a cumulative

---

[70] This is Proposition 3.3 according to which the plural formulation of the existence and identity postulates for rigid embodiments are inconsistent with the existence of more than one object.

[71] See Jacinto and Cotnoir (2019) for a construction of models for the iterative conception of embodiment.

hierarchy: no sense is to be made, for example, of a rigid embodiment of *all* embodiments as they exemplify some attribute. For that embodiment would have be involved in the explanation of what that object is: the embodiment would itself be one of the embodiments the attribute is supposed to unify. But that would not, of course, be a genuine explanation. Thus, the rationale for the postulate of iterative existence is the general thought that the immediate parts of a rigid embodiment are prior to them, and thus they are generated in stages.

One more consequence of the proposal is that all classes are improper: there are no proper classes. Instead, since all classes are formed at some level of the cumulative hierarchy, they behave like sets. They submit in fact to the axioms of ZF, which with the exception of extensionality, translate into constraints on the width and height of the cumulative hierarchy. This is, in fact, the import of the appendix of Caplan, Tillman, and Reeder (2010). The justification of extensionality appealed to the characterization of class as a rigid embodiment of some objects as they exist. Notice that the status of the axiom of choice becomes entangled with the status of plural choice. Whether there is a choice function for a family of nonempty sets turns on whether we are able to select one member of each plurality involved in the rigid embodiment for each set in the family to form a plurality with exactly one member in common with each of them.

One may still wonder how to formalize the iterative conception of classes conceived as rigid embodiments that emerges. One way to proceed is to adapt the strategy outlined in Button (2021, Appendix A) in order to provide an axiomatization of set theory in terms exclusively of the relation of *immediate part*. Define a class A to be *potent* if and only if whenever x is an individual without immediate parts or whenever x is a subclass of some immediate part of a, then x is an immediate part of a, that is:

$$\forall x(\neg \exists y \, y \ll x \vee \exists Y(CY \wedge x \subseteq Y \wedge Y \in A) \rightarrow x \in A).$$

Let $\#A$ be the class of individuals and subclasses of immediate parts of A, *if it exists*, and call a class H a *history* if every immediate part x of H verifies $x = \#(x \cap H)$. Finally, and following Button (2021), we write that a class S is a *level* if, and only if, $S = \#H$ for some history H. The axioms of set theory now include:

$$\forall X(CX \rightarrow (\exists S \, Level(S) \wedge A \subseteq V)). \qquad \text{Stratification}$$

That is, every class is a subclass of some level. We may supplement the framework with a further axiom designed to guarantee that whenever some objects are immediate parts of a level, they form a class:

$$\exists S \, (Level(S) \forall y(y \prec xx \rightarrow y \ll S) \rightarrow \exists x \, x = xx/E. \qquad \text{Separation}$$

The axioms of separation, union, and foundation are immediate consequences of the hypothesis that classes are formed in stages of the cumulative hierarchy.[72] To secure the pair and power set axioms, we would adopt the hypothesis that there is no last stage in the hierarchy.[73] And the further hypothesis that there is a limit level without an immediate predecessor delivers a justification of the axiom of infinity.[74] The axiom of replacement would be derivable from the further hypothesis that no class is cofinal with the cumulative hierarchy, that is, that there is no unbounded map from a set into the hierarchy of stages.

6 Conclusion

We have taken the position that the relation of part to whole applies across ontological categories; classes are, at the very least, parts of themselves. It is a further question whether classes ever have parts other than themselves, and we have explored two different stances on which they do. One identifies the parts of a class with its subclasses, while the other takes the parts of a class to include its members. Each perspective results in a different mereological reconstruction of the theory of classes.

How should we decide between the two broad outlooks? We doubt the issue may be settled by reflection on linguistic evidence or on the common judgments we are inclined to make when asked to list the parts of a class. Ordinary judgments often pull us in different directions, and the views under consideration turn out to be selective with respect to which ordinary judgments should be preserved and which should be dismissed as nonliteral or perhaps as a figure of speech. The Main Thesis respects the judgment that subclasses are parts of classes but it dismisses the judgment that classes are composed of their members as nonliteral or as a figure of speech. One version of Hierarchical Composition requires one to take the latter judgment at face value and to cast doubt upon the former. Liberal Hierarchical Composition appears to be able to take a broader class of ordinary judgments at face value, but at the cost of a distinction between a relation of immediate part and the more familiar relation of part to whole.

Nor will the prospects of a mereological foundation for class theory tilt the scales in one direction rather than another. Unless the relation of member is itself viewed as a species of part, there is no reason to expect a *direct* reduction

---

[72] This is fact (1) in Proposition 7.1 in Button (2021).

[73] This is fact (2) in Proposition 7.1 in Button (2021).

[74] This is fact (3) in Proposition 7.1 in Button (2021).

of member to the relation of part to whole. Perhaps we should not completely discard the prospects of a mereological facsimile of the relation of member; witness, for example, the relation of pseudomember that Forrest (2002b) identifies against the background of Heyting mereology, but we should not bank on it either. Each broad outlook of the mereology of classes approaches the situation differently.

Subscribers to the Main Thesis circumvent the lack of a direct reduction of member to part by appeal to a singleton operation, and they differ with respect to their attitude to that operation. While some prefer to take a structuralist approach to singletons, others seek a reduction to more familiar operations. Both reactions face difficulties of their own. If one is prepared to take a structuralist stance on the singleton operation, one may as well provide a structuralist account of membership and avoid the detour through singletons. The choice would be between the thesis that classes are fusions of whatever objects are the output of an operation with certain structural features, and the thesis that classes are whatever objects play a role in a certain membership structure. It is not clear how to weigh the advantages of each tack.

On the other hand, those who seek a reduction of the singleton operation face the threat of inconsistency: they must restrict the axioms of Classical Extensional Mereology to accommodate the existence of a total injective map from objects to mereological atoms. The challenge is to find a restriction that is neither ad hoc or unmotivated nor unable to deliver a sufficiently rich and varied domain of classes.

Proponents of Hierarchical Composition take member to be a species of part: *immediate part*. They face a different limitative result as they must acknowledge that member, qua immediate part, is not itself directly definable in terms of part. But this observation has different significance for different theorists. Some authors, for example, Forrest (2002b), opt for the development of a mereological surrogate for member defined in terms of nonimmediate part, whereas others seek to subsume class theory within a more general theory of immediate part. The first route requires their proponents to rely on the assumption that the universe of individuals is sufficiently rich and varied to support mereological surrogates for a variety of pure classes, whereas the second requires one to repurpose mereology primarily as a theory of immediate part, for example, Caplan, Tillman, and Reeder (2010), whose formal behavior is significantly different from that of the relation of part to whole. This is, of course, feasible and the formal framework that results is one in which one may indeed interpret the theory of classes. But while that may come as no surprise once one reflects on the formal features of the relation of immediate part, it is difficult to avoid the impression that we changed the subject when we introduced hierarchical mereology and offered a reduction of part in terms of immediate part.

Neither linguistic evidence nor the prospects of a mereological foundation seem, in the end, decisive considerations for one outlook rather than the other, and they should be weighed against considerations of explanatory power and antecedent commitments on the nature of the part-to-whole relation.

What may predispose theorists toward one or another view of the mereology of classes is an antecedent broad conception of the part-to-whole relation. Compositional monists for whom the part-to-whole relation exemplifies the structure of a Boolean algebra will generally fall in line with the Main Thesis; the structural parallels between subclass and part will incline them to identify the former as a special case of the latter.[75] Matters will be different for theorists inclined to discern a hierarchical structure in a whole. For they will have the resources to assimilate the member relation to that of immediate part. When combined with compositional pluralism, one may even be in a position to allow for a multiplicity of senses in which something may be a member of class: subclasses are parts of a class in a different way in which members are parts of a class. What we have learned in the course of this investigation is that each theorist faces further choice points once they situate themselves in the debate over what are the parts of a class, and one further dimension of evaluation concerns whether or not the choices ultimately give rise to a powerful and attractive theory of classes.

We have isolated a further point of contact between the mereology of classes and the foundations of set theory, one which is independent from the ambition to identify sets with wholes composed out of parts. For even if one remains agnostic as to whether sets are special cases of classes, one may conceive of proper classes, that is, classes that are not sets, as wholes ultimately composed of singletons. The mereological interpretation of proper classes emerges as an attractive solution to the problem of proper classes in set theory: whatever the nature of sets, the identification of proper classes with sums of singletons allows one to motivate a fruitful distinction between the element–set relation and the relation a member bears to a class. Proper classes are conceived as parts of the set- theoretic universe, which, unlike sets, are not formed at stages of the cumulative hierarchy. The crucial question, however, is

---

[75] David Lewis takes the part-to-whole relation to exemplify the structure of a *complete* Boolean algebra because he embraces the axiom of fusion, but there is room in principle for a proponent of the Main Thesis to restrict fusion.

whether there is a principled reason to preclude proper classes from being elements, and the difficulties associated with a negative answer to that question are not dissimilar to the dilemma we encountered when we attempted to combine the Main Thesis with a perfectly general theory of singleton against the background of CEM.

References

Armstrong, David M. 1991. "Classes Are States of Affairs." *Mind* 100 (2): 189–201.

Armstrong, David M. 1995. "Reply to Rosen." *Australasian Journal of Philosophy* 73 (4): 626–628.

Barwise, John, and Lawrence Moss. 1996. *Vicious Circles: On the Mathematics of Circular Phenomena, CSLI-Lecture Notes*. Center for the Study of Language and Information at Stanford University.

Bell, John L. 2004. "Whole and Part in Mathematics." *Axiomathes* 14 (4): 285–294.

Bigelow, John. 1993. "Sets Are Haecceities." In John Bacon, Keith Campbell, and Lloyd Reinhardt (Eds.), *Ontology, Causality and Mind*, 73–96. Cambridge University Press.

Boolos, George. 1984. "To Be Is to Be a Value of a Variable (or to Be Some Values of Some Variables)." *The Journal of Philosophy* 81 (8): 430.

1985. "Nominalist Platonism." *The Philosophical Review* 94 (3): 327–344.

Burgess, John P. 2004. "E Pluribus Unum: Plural Logic and Set Theory." *Philosophia Mathematica* 12(3): 193–221.

Burgess, John P. 2015. "Lewis on Mereology and Set Theory." In Barry Loewer and Jonathan Schaffer (Eds.), *A Companion to David Lewis*, 459–469. John Wiley & Sons, Ltd.

Button, Tim. 2021. "Level Theory, Part 1: Axiomatizing the Bare Idea of a Cumulative Hierarchy of Sets." *The Bulletin of Symbolic Logic* 27 (4): 436–460.

Caplan, Ben, Chris Tillman, and Pat Reeder. 2010. "Parts of Singletons." *Journal of Philosophy* 107(10): 501–533.

Cartwright, Richard L., 2001. "A Question about Sets." In Alex Byrne, Robert Stalnaker, and Ralph Wedgwood (Eds.), *Fact and Value: Essays on Ethics and Metaphysics for Judith Jarvis Thomson*, 29–46. Massachusetts Institute of Technology Press.

Casati, Roberto, and Achille C. Varzi. 1999. *Parts and Places: The Structures of Spatial Representation*. Massachusetts Institute of Technology Press.

Cotnoir, Aaron J. 2010. "Anti-Symmetry and Non-Extensional Mereology." *The Philosophical Quarterly* 60 (239): 396–405.

Cotnoir, Aaron J., and Achille C. Varzi. 2019. "Natural Axioms for Classical Mereology." *The Review of Symbolic Logic* 12 (1): 201–208.

2021. *Mereology*. Oxford University Press.

Eberle, Rolf A. 1970. *Nominalistic Systems*. Vol. 30. Synthese Library. Springer Science & Business Media.

Fairchild, Maegan. 2017. "A Paradox of Matter and Form." *Thought: A Journal of Philosophy* 6 (1): 33–42.

Fine, Kit. 1992. "Aristotle on Matter." *Mind* 101 (401): 35–58.

——— 1999. "Things and Their Parts." *Midwest Studies In Philosophy* 23 (1)23: 61–74.

——— 2010. "Towards a Theory of Part." *Journal of Philosophy* 107 (11): 559–589.

Florio, Salvatore, and Øystein Linnebo. 2021. *The Many and the One: A Philosophical Study of Plural Logic*. Oxford University Press.

Forrest, Peter. 2002a. "Sets as Mereological Tropes." *Metaphysica* 3 (1): 5–8.

——— 2002b. "Nonclassical Mereology and Its Application to Sets." *Notre Dame Journal of Formal Logic* 43 (2): 79–94.

Gödel, Kurt. 1947. "What Is Cantor's Continuum Problem?" *The American Mathematical Monthly* 54 (9): 515–525.

Goodman, Jeremy. 2022. "Matter and Mereology." https://jeremy-goodman.com/MatterMereology.pdf.

Hamkins, Joel David, and Makoto Kikuchi. 2016. "Set-Theoretic Mereology." *Logic and Logical Philosophy* 25 (3): 285–308.

Hellman, Geoffrey. 1989. *Mathematics without Numbers: Towards a Modal-Structural Interpretation*. Clarendon Press.

——— 1996. "Structuralism without Structures." *Philosophia Mathematica* 4 (2): 100–123.

Horsten, Leon. 2016. "Absolute Infinity in Class Theory and in Theology." In Francesca Boccuni and Andrea Sereni (Eds.), *Objectivity, Realism, and Proof*, Boston Studies in the Philosophy and History of Science, 318: 103–122. Springer International Publishing.

Horsten, Leon, and Philip Welch. 2016. "Reflecting on Absolute Infinity." *Journal of Philosophy* 113 (2): 89–111.

Hovda, Paul. 2009. "What Is Classical Mereology?" *Journal of Philosophical Logic* 38 (1): 55–82.

Incurvati, Luca. 2020. *Conceptions of Set and the Foundations of Mathematics*. Cambridge University Press.

Jacinto, Bruno, and Aaron J. Cotnoir. 2019. "Models for Hylomorphism." *Journal of Philosophical Logic* 48 (5): 909–955.

Johnston, Mark. 2006. "Hylomorphism." *The Journal of Philosophy* 103 (12): 652–698.

Kanamori, Akihiro. 2003. "The Empty Set, the Singleton, and the Ordered Pair." *The Bulletin of Symbolic Logic* 9 (3): 273–298.

Koslicki, Kathrin. 2008. *The Structure of Objects*. Oxford University Press on Demand.

Leśniewski, Stanisław. 1927. "O Podstawach Matematyki [On the Foundations of Mathematics]." *Przeglad Filozoficzny* 30: 164–206.

  1999. "Foundations of the General Theory of Sets. i." *Filozofia Nauki* 7 (3–4): 173–208.

Lewis, David. 1970. "Nominalistic Set Theory." *Noûs*, 4 (3): 225–240.

  1986. *On the Plurality of Worlds*. Wiley Blackwell.

  1991. *Parts of Classes*. Wiley Blackwell.

  1993. "Mathematics Is Megethology." *Philosophia Mathematica* 1 (1): 3–23.

Maddy, Penelope. 1983. "Proper Classes." *The Journal of Symbolic Logic* 48 (1): 113–139.

McCarthy, Timothy. 2015. "A Note on Unrestricted Composition." *Thought: A Journal of Philosophy* 4 (3): 202–211.

McDaniel, Kris. 2009. "Structure-Making." *Australasian Journal of Philosophy* 87 (2): 251–274.

McGee, Vann. 1997. "How We Learn Mathematical Language." *The Philosophical Review* 106 (1): 35–68.

Menzel, Christopher. 2014. "Wide Sets, ZFCU, and the Iterative Conception." *Journal of Philosophy* 111 (2): 57–83.

Mormann, Thomas. 2012. "On the Mereological Structure of Complex States of Affairs." *Synthese* 187 (2): 403–418.

  2013. "Heyting Mereology as a Framework for Spatial Reasoning." *Axiomathes* 23 (1): 137–164.

Oliver, Alex, and Timothy Smiley. 2006. "What Are Sets and What Are They For?" *Philosophical Perspectives* 20 (1): 123–155.

  2018. "Cantorian Set Theory." *The Bulletin of Symbolic Logic* 24 (4): 393–451.

Rosen, Gideon. 1995. "Armstrong on Classes as States of Affairs." *Australasian Journal of Philosophy* 73 (4): 613–625.

Russell, Jeffrey Sanford. 2016. "Indefinite Divisibility." *Inquiry* 59 (3): 239–263.

Shapiro, Stewart. 1991. *Foundations without Foundationalism: A Case for Second-Order Logic*. Vol. 17. Clarendon Press.

Simons, Peter. 1987. *Parts: A Study in Ontology*. Clarendon Press.

Tarski, Alfred. 1983. "Foundations of the Geometry of Solids." In John Corcoran (Ed.), *Logic, Semantics, Metamathematics*, 24–29. Hackett.

Urbaniak, Rafal. 2014. *Leśniewski's Systems of Logic and Foundations of Mathematics*. Springer.

Uzquiano, Gabriel. 2003. "Plural Quantification and Classes." *Philosophia Mathematica* 11 (1): 67–81.

2015a. "Varieties of Indefinite Extensibility." *Notre Dame Journal of Formal Logic* 56 (1): 147–166.

2015b. "A Neglected Resolution of Russell's Paradox of Propositions." *The Review of Symbolic Logic* 8 (2): 328–344.

2018. "Groups: Toward a Theory of Plural Embodiment." *Journal of Philosophy* 115 (8): 423–432.

Zermelo, Ernst. 1930. "Über Grenzzahlen und Mengenbereiche: Neue Untersuchungen über die Grundlagen der Mengenlehre." *Fundamenta Mathematicae* 16: 29–47.

.

Cambridge Elements $\equiv$

The Philosophy of Mathematics

Penelope Rush
University of Tasmania

From the time Penny Rush completed her thesis in the philosophy of mathematics (2005), she has worked continuously on themes around the realism/anti-realism divide and the nature of mathematics. Her edited collection *The Metaphysics of Logic* (Cambridge University Press, 2014), and forthcoming essay "Metaphysical Optimism" (*Philosophy Supplement*), highlight a particular interest in the idea of reality itself and curiosity and respect as important philosophical methodologies.

Stewart Shapiro
The Ohio State University

Stewart Shapiro is the O'Donnell Professor of Philosophy at The Ohio State University, a Distinguished Visiting Professor at the University of Connecticut, and a Professorial Fellow at the University of Oslo. His major works include *Foundations without Foundationalism* (1991), *Philosophy of Mathematics: Structure and Ontology* (1997), *Vagueness in Context* (2006), and *Varieties of Logic* (2014). He has taught courses in logic, philosophy of mathematics, metaphysics, epistemology, philosophy of religion, Jewish philosophy, social and political philosophy, and medical ethics.

About the Series

This Cambridge Elements series provides an extensive overview of the philosophy of mathematics in its many and varied forms. Distinguished authors will provide an up-to-date summary of the results of current research in their fields and give their own take on what they believe are the most significant debates influencing research, drawing original conclusions.

Cambridge Elements ≡

The Philosophy of Mathematics

Elements in the Series

A full series listing is available at: www.cambridge.org/EPM

Printed in the United States
by Baker & Taylor Publisher Services